THE
DRIED
FLOWER
ARRANGER

THE DRIED FLOWER ARRANGER

ALEX MACCORMICK

MICHAEL O'MARA BOOKS LIMITED

FOR DELPHINE MACCORMICK
WITH LOVE AND THANKS

Note
The author and publishers would like to
acknowledge the help of
Jane Durbridge, who made this book possible.

First published in paperback in 1993 by
Michael O'Mara Books Limited

First published in 1992 by
Michael O'Mara Books Limited,
9 Lion Yard, Tremadoc Road, London SW4 7NQ

A CIP catalogue record for this book
is available from the British Library

ISBN 1–85479–186–9 (hardback)
ISBN 1–85479–931–2 (paperback)

Art director and designer: Jeanette Collins
Typeset by Florencetype Ltd, Stoodleigh, Devon
Printed and bound in Hong Kong by Paramount Printing Co., Ltd

CONTENTS

ACKNOWLEDGMENTS 6

INTRODUCTION 7

BASIC EQUIPMENT 13

BASIC TECHNIQUES 14

THE SEASONS 22

HARVEST THANKSGIVING 30

CHRISTMAS 32

PARTY TIME 42

PRESENTS 44

VALENTINE'S DAY 52

EASTER 54

SIDETABLES, SIDEBOARDS AND
    WINDOWSILLS 56

DINING TABLE CENTREPIECES 80

POSIES 84

TREES 88

SWAG 94

GARLANDS 96

HANGING BUNCH 102

PEDESTALS 104

WALLS: PLAQUES, BASKETS AND
    MIRRORS 110

ROSE BALL 120

MINIATURES 122

ROSE POTS 124

FIREPLACES 126

MANTELPIECES 130

EXOTICA 134

LIST OF SUPPLIERS 142

INDEX 143

ACKNOWLEDGMENTS

The author and publishers would particularly like to thank
Jane Durbridge and Nigel Wooller of Parterre Flowers Ltd,
8 Marylebone Passage, London W1N 7HE (tel: 071–323–1623),
without whose kind help and invaluable expertise this book would not have been possible.
The author and publishers are also very grateful for generous assistance from the following:
Aromaround; Maria de Botello; Simon Brown; Helga Hislop; Rosalind Quinn (Director of Sales)
and the London Marriott Hotel, Grosvenor Square, London W1; Ercole and the staff at McQueen's;
Joan Mungall of Patio; Caroline Smail and Juliet Willis;
Henrietta Thompson of Wulfsohn & James; and Stephen Woodhams.

In addition the author wishes to thank
David Roberts, Lesley O'Mara, editor Catherine Taylor and the staff of Michael O'Mara Books;
art director and designer Jeanette Collins; and the photographer Derrick E. Witty.

The photographs, other than those listed below,
were specially taken by Derrick E. Witty and styled by Jeanette Collins.
The credits by the side of the pictures indicate the arranger.
The author and publishers acknowledge kind permission to reproduce
copyright illustrations from the following:
Jeanette Collins, pp. 67, 100–1; EWA, pp. 120, 136; The Garden Picture Library,
pp. 23, 129, 135; Susan Griggs Agency, © Simon McBride, pp. 24–5, 83, 93, 109;
Robert Harding Picture Library, © Fin Costello, pp. 26–7;
Jerry Harpur, p. 6 (designed by Kitty Waddell); IPC Magazines 1991 / Robert Harding, p. 33;
S & O Mathews, pp. 2, 58; National Magazine Co. and the Editor of *She*, p. 37;
Peter Rauter, pp. 29, 30, 88; Juliet Willis, pp. 42–3, 130.

INTRODUCTION

Flowers are a source of great joy, which is no doubt why since ancient times they have played an important part in marking the special events in our lives. From birth and childhood successes through courtship, weddings, birthdays, anniversaries and seasonal celebrations until our departure from this world, we 'say it with flowers'.

While everyone appreciates the short-lived delights of fresh flowers, few these days can afford the luxury of buying, arranging and clearing them away on a regular basis. Dried flower arrangements, however, provide an enduring pleasure which can last for years, which means that they are not only good value for money in the long run but can also save a great deal of time.

Over the last few years an ever broader range of dried flowers and plant material has become widely available. Gone are the days when the words 'dried flower arrangement' conjured up ghastly visions of moth-eaten pampas grass, some flat, dusty leaves and a few pallid, unrecognizable flowers lurking spookily in a gloomy corner. Now, as you can see in this book, there are endless exciting ideas for enhancing any room to suit your taste and needs.

One reason why dried flowers not

only look so much

fresher and prettier than they used to

but have also become an

indispensable decorative feature

is the number of ways

in which material is now dried.

DRYING METHODS

No single method is guaranteed foolproof in successfully preserving different types of material. Success depends not only on extracting all moisture but also on picking the material at the right time, on the temperature at the time and on the humidity. A few rules, however, apply to all methods:

1 All stalks must be cut cleanly and at an angle with sharp secateurs or scissors.
2 Avoid cutting before the morning dew has dried off, after rainfall and in the mid-day sun.
3 Cut flowers just before they come into full bloom, when the blooms or heads feel 'firm'. Spikes of flowers like delphinium, larkspur (*Consolida* sp), foxgloves (*Digitalis*), lupins (*Lupinus*), etc., should be gathered when the lower buds are flowering, but the top ones have not yet burst open.
4 Avoid gathering imperfect or damaged material.

AIR DRYING

This is the simplest, most commonly used method and is successful for a wide variety of flowers, herbs, gourds, grasses, leafy branches, seedheads and cereals. All you need is a dry, cool (10°C/50°F) room with circulating air such as a spare room, an attic/loft or cellar, a garage or shed – even an unheated airing or linen cupboard.

Most flowers can be dried by hanging them upside down in spread out bunches loosely tied with raffia or string. Stagger the positions of the flower heads and, to help prevent rot, remove the lower leaves or any rose thorns before tying them. You can hang them from wall hooks or from poles or wires rigged at least 6 in (15 cm) from the ceiling or top of the cupboard. Suitable plants for this method include Chinese lantern/bladder cherry (*Physalis alkekengi franchetii*), roses, *Helichrysum*, larkspur (*Consolida* sp), *Helipterum*, statice (*Limonium sinuatum*), yarrow (*Achillea* sp), *Alchemilla mollis*, mimosa/wattle (*Acacia*) and golden rod (*Solidago* sp).

Most grasses, bamboos, fungi and leafy branches dry well when laid flat on an absorbent surface such as cardboard, newspaper or even wooden floorboards. Space out the material to allow air to circulate. Leaves shrivel a little, but retain their colour and natural shape on the stalk, which they do not do if they are hung upside down or are dried upright. Other plants suitable for this method include lavender (*Lavendula spica*) and hogweed (*Heracleum sphondylium*).

The seedheads of some grasses, particularly pampas grass (*Cortaderia selloana*) and bulrushes, need to be sealed by spraying them with hair lacquer or similar fixative before drying, otherwise they will break up.

Drying upright suits other plants. Tall grasses and seedheads such as pampas (*Cortaderia selloana*), dock (*Rumex* sp), onion seedheads (*Allium*), sea lavender (*Limonium* sp), bulrushes and *Chenopodium* dry well when left standing in an empty vase. However, flowers such as hybrid delphiniums, hydrangeas, *Gypsophila* and mimosa/wattle (*Acacia*) are best when stood in about 2 in (5 cm) of water and left until all the water has been taken up and the plants are completely dry.

All moss and lichen is best dried in single layers on a bed of crumpled newspaper in a box or on a tray.

A rack made of coarse-gauge chicken wire is the best method for air-drying heavy-headed plant material such as globe artichokes (*Cynara scolymus*), large onion seedheads (*Allium*), *Protea*, lotus flowers (fruit) (*Nelumbo lucifera*), and large thistles like *Carlina acaulis*. Each plant is slotted through a hole in the mesh with enough room beneath to allow the stalk to hang freely.

DESICCANTS

Drying agents such as silica gel, borax and sand, or a mixture of all three, can be used to extract the moisture from leaves and flowers, thus preserving their colour and form. This method is both time-consuming and costly to do on a large scale, so it is best suited to small quantities. Flower heads should be wired first (see pp. 18–20) because they become too brittle to do so afterwards and space is too limited to accommodate long stalks.

Either powdered borax or alum can be mixed with fine silver sand, using 3 parts of the chemical to 2 parts sand. Place a layer of the mixture about $^1/_2$ in (1.3 cm) thick in a lidded container such as a biscuit tin. Place the leaves or flowers on top and then cover them completely with another layer of the mixture sprinkled delicately on top. Ease the mixture between petals and into crevices with a small paintbrush. Cover and leave for 10 days before checking that the material is firm and dry. If so, remove the flowers or leaves at once. To re-use the mixture, dry it out at a low heat in an oven and store it in an airtight container.

Silica gel is available from a chemist either in the form of white crystals or, more usefully, as blue colour-indicator crystals, which turn pink once they have absorbed moisture. Crush the colour-indicator crystals with a mortar and pestle to less than half their original size. Then follow the procedure for the borax/alum and sand mixture, but only wait 2 days before checking that the plant material is firm to the touch and the crystals have turned pink. Remove the flowers or leaves immediately. Again, the crystals can be dried in an oven at a low heat until they turn blue again and then stored in an airtight container for re-use.

FREEZE DRYING

This is the latest method increasingly used not only for herbs and vegetables but also for flowers by some commercial growers and suppliers. Moisture is extracted from plant material at very low temperatures, allowing flowers, for instance, to retain their original colour and form, many fully open (see p. 6). Some critics feel the results look as lifeless as porcelain, but plant material dried in this way will doubtless gain wider popularity when it becomes cheaper and more widely available. It is not, however, currently a feasible method to use at home because of the equipment and processes involved.

GLYCERINE

A few flowers, including heathers (*Erica* sp), hydrangeas, Jerusalem sage (*Phlomis fructicosa*) and bells of Ireland (*Molucella*), can be preserved using glycerine, but on the whole the best results are achieved with foliage. Although the colours of foliage usually change to khaki or a shade of brown, this is not always a disadvantage: for instance, green magnolia leaves retain their sheen and emerge a rich, dark greeny brown, almost black. Leaves also remain pliable, which can be handy. Amongst the other foliage which can be dried successfully by this method are copper beech (*Fagus sylvatica 'Cuprea'*), pin oak (*Quercus palustris*), eucalyptus, laurel (*Prunus laurocerasus*), ferns, ivy (*Hedera* sp), and *Choisya* and *Mahonia* leaves. Gather foliage in summer whilst the sap is still rising.

The first time you use this method, start with only a few stems of foliage or flowers because they use up a lot of glycerine mixture.

Cut the base of each stalk at a sharp angle, so that the plant will take up the mixture speedily and remove leaves from the bottom 5 in (12.5 cm) of stem. Hardwood stems should be hammered and split. Stand the plant material in water for a couple of hours so that it is refreshed. Make the glycerine solution using 40% glycerine and 60% very hot water. Stand the plant stems in a container with 3–4 in (7.5–10 cm) of the mixture in the bottom. Make sure that all stalks are safely supported and that no leaves touch the mixture. Leave the container and its contents in a cool, dark place for about 10 days or more, but start checking for colour change and dryness after 1 week.

Large individual leaves or sprays can be preserved by totally immersing them in a container of 50% glycerine and 50% very hot water until the colour changes completely. Then remove and wash them using a mild detergent before laying them flat on sheets of newspaper to dry.

MICROWAVING

Drying plant material in microwave ovens is not common in Great Britain, but is more popular elsewhere. The amount of material which can be dried at any one time is obviously limited, but it is a quick method suitable for such compact plants as carnations (*Dianthus* sp), roses, pansies (*Viola* sp), sunflowers (*Helianthus* sp), chrysanthemums, asters, zinnias, daffodils (*Narcissus* sp), pine cones and also individual leaves and leaf sprays. Fresh, half-open flowers are best.

The most common basic method is to cut the stem of, for instance, a carnation below the base of the head, insert a wooden toothpick into the base and then trim the toothpick to about $1/2$ in (1.3 cm). Place a layer of blue colour-indicator silica gel crystals (see Desiccants above) in a large cup, stand the carnation upright in the crystals and, with the aid of a small paintbrush to ease crystals into crevices, gently cover the flower completely. Place the cup uncovered in a microwave oven on High for about 1 minute 20 seconds (650 watt-power oven). Remove a few crystals to check if the petals are still soft; if they are, re-cover the flower with crystals and microwave it in 15-second bursts until the flower is dry. Pour the silica gel out into a bowl and stand the carnation with its base in the hot crystals for 3 minutes. The crystals turn pink when they absorb moisture. Once all the crystals have been carefully brushed off the flower, it is ready for wiring as you would a rose head (see p. 18).

Rose leaves and stems, for instance, can be preserved by immersing them in 50% glycerine mixed with 50% very hot water for 1 hour, drying them carefully with absorbent paper and then microwaving them on a plate on High for 30 seconds. They will keep their colour.

The timing for other plant material depends on how porous it is.

OVEN DRYING

Fan-assisted electric ovens are most suitable for this method because Aga-type ovens tend to be too hot and gas ovens generate too much moisture. The amount of material which can be dried at any one time is fairly limited and plants shrink, sometimes quite considerably, though they retain their colour and original form fairly well. A wide variety of plants may be dried using this method, but it is particularly successful with compact varieties such as marigolds (*Tagetes* sp), chrysanthemums, cornflowers (*Centaurea cyranus*) and zinnias as well as pine cones.

The main guidelines to bear in mind are that all material must be dried at a very low temperature over many hours and that flowers are best dried upright, slotted through the holes of a wire mesh rack with room for the stalks to hang freely. The time required for drying depends on how dense or porous the plant material is, but it is best to check the contents of the oven regularly since many oven thermostats are unreliable.

PRESSING

This method of preservation is nowadays seldom used for dried flower arrangements because the results are two dimensional, although original colours are effectively retained. Pressed flowers are ideal, though, for making into pictures, for decorating lampshades, boxes, packets of pot pourri, etc.

Amongst the plants suitable for pressing are pansies (*Viola* sp), lace-cap hydrangea (*Hydrangea paniculata*), lilies, freesia, anemones, hellebore, marguerites (*Compositae* sp), primula, snowdrops (*Galanthus* sp), clematis, ferns and tree leaves or sprays. Avoid fleshy or very three-dimensional plants.

A home-made or shop-bought flower press will give the best results. The former can be made of two heavy hardwood or thick plywood boards. Drill matching holes in the corners of both boards to accept four bolts with securing wing nuts. The flowers or leaves are placed between two layers of blotting or absorbent paper, which is then sandwiched between two layers of thick cardboard. The whole pile is then inserted between the wooden boards, the screws of which are tightened to press the contents flat.

Larger pieces of foliage can be pressed between sheets of newspaper placed under a little used area of carpet, whilst small flower heads can be dried between sheets of blotting paper placed under a couple of large, heavy books.

The length of time material takes to dry depends on how porous or dense it is, but check after about 10 days.

HANDY HINTS AND GENERAL INFORMATION

Rather like a cookery book, the detailed recipes given for the arrangements illustrated include a list of plant ingredients and quantities plus a list of equipment needed for each particular arrangement. Also like a cookery book, it is expected that many readers will use these recipes as a starting point from which to invent variations rather than as a set of unbreakable rules.

THE NAMES OF PLANTS are, wherever possible, listed in the recipes first by their common name and then by their Latin name. (The abbreviation 'sp' is short for 'species' or family). There are many different-looking types of *Limonium*, *Helichrysum* or *Helipterum*, for instance, just as there are many different Smiths in a telephone directory, so gradually learning both names will help you identify and buy the right ingredients. Within the text plants are referred to by whichever name they are most commonly called. The colours mentioned before the names are intended as an aid to identification of plants in the photographs, which may be dyed or naturally that shade.

QUANTITIES for each plant ingredient listed in a recipe are generally given in bunches, which will vary in size from shop to shop, but in the United Kingdom there are, for instance, about 18–20 roses per bunch. If you are in any doubt about whether the quantities specified will be sufficient for your particular needs then take this book to a florist and check with him or her.

WHEN YOU CANNOT FIND WHAT YOU WANT substitute a plant of roughly similar shape, colour or texture. Some exotica can be tricky to come by, but be inventive. Do not ignore a particular arrangement merely because the precise ingredients are not to hand.

COST can be kept down by using one or more good, less expensive 'fillers' such as cereals, grasses, herbs, sea lavender (*Limonium* sp), *Gypsophila*, love-in-a-mist (*Nigella*), etc., to provide up to two-thirds of the arrangement.

THE BEST TIME TO BUY dried flowers is from September through to Christmas in Europe and

North America, and from March onwards in the southern hemisphere. However, there is now a worldwide trade in dried plant material, and shops are usually only short of stock in the weeks following Christmas.

CHOOSING COLOURS can be a headache, but a helpful guideline is to pick out the two or three main colours in the relevant room and then add one sympathetic colour which is not. For instance, if the living room has beige walls, peach/pink curtains and a blue sofa then use such ingredients as pinky beige grasses, blue delphiniums and lavender *plus* maroon roses. The extra colour prevents the arrangement from fading into the background. But do not let this suggestion inhibit you – even guidelines are meant to be broken sometimes. Also do not be afraid of judiciously mixing dyed and natural plants.

TO PRESERVE THE COLOURS of flowers and other plant material, keep arrangements away from windows and out of bright sunlight. If you want a long-lasting arrangement for a windowsill, use naturally pale plant ingredients with interesting shapes and textures (see the Exotic Shades of White recipe, for instance, on p. 137). Alternatively, you can use strong colours and resign yourself to the fact that the arrangement will lose its sparkle within a year.

LIFELIKE ARRANGEMENTS are more likely to result from following these few simple guidelines. First, never try to make an arrangement look tidy and totally symmetrical because it will not look natural – it will look dead instead of alive. Secondly, while you are arranging dried plants, step back periodically to check that the balance and shape are pleasing from all angles. Thirdly, never leave any dry foam or wire showing in a completed arrangement – if necessary, cover it with moss or a small left-over. Fourthly, remember that plants on wire 'stems' (see pp. 18–20) can be bent and therefore look more natural than ones with rigid stalks.

CLEANING an arrangement is never entirely without hazard, but the simplest way of removing dust is with a hair-dryer held about 2 ft (60 cm) away so that warm air blows gently over it. Glycerine-dried leaves may occasionally be wiped with a damp piece of cottonwool.

MCQUEEN'S

The aim of this book is to present some attractive and imaginative ways of using dried flowers – a number are simple enough for a child to do, while others are more complex. I hope that it will prove a source of inspiration and enjoyment for many years to come.

BASIC EQUIPMENT

Dry foam block, ball, cone, etc.
Stub/florists' wire: ordinary and long; fine, medium and coarse gauge
Reel wire, various colours
Reel of rose wire
Gutta-percha tape, various colours
Serrated florists' scissors
Wire-cutters } sometimes combined
Pliers
Chicken wire, coarse and fine gauge
Staple gun
Hot glue gun
Cold glue (Copydex type)
Raffia, natural and other colours
Ribbons: paper, silk, velvet, etc.

Lengths of cane
Reel of adhesive tape
Plaster of Paris powder or quick-drying cement
Florists' plastic spikes/prongs
Adhesive clay (or similar) on tape
Secateurs
Wire wreath frame
Vine (or similar) circle/garland base
Florists' knife

BASIC TECHNIQUES

JEANETTE COLLINS

PREPARING CONTAINERS AND BASES

FLAT-BOTTOMED SAUCERS OR CIRCULAR DISHES

EQUIPMENT
Dry-foam blocks – 1 or more, depending on the size of the container; reel of adhesive tape; scissors; strong cold glue; sharp knife.

METHOD
Sculpt a mound of dry foam. If necessary use 2 or more blocks of foam held tightly together, side by side, with adhesive tape. Stick the flat side of the foam to the saucer or dish with glue.

BASKETS

INGREDIENTS
Ordinary green 'sack' moss (*Mnium*) or sphagnum moss – 1 medium packet.

EQUIPMENT
Reel of narrow adhesive tape; dry-foam block(s) – enough to overfill the basket; stub/florists' wire – 1 piece medium gauge; scissors; sharp knife; pliers.

METHOD
Use the base of the basket to indent 1 or more blocks of foam with its shape.

Using the indent mark as a guide, cut the block(s) of foam to fit in the bottom of the basket as snugly as possible.

If required, place on top of the block(s) of foam a second (or more) piece(s) cut to form A MOUND 1 in (2.5 cm) above the rim of the basket.

To secure the foam in the basket, take a length of stub/florists' wire, loop one end to form an eye (using pliers, if necessary), thread the adhesive tape through this eye and – using the wire as a needle – thread the tape through a cane on the inner rim of the basket.

Pull sufficient tape through to cross the basket diagonally, thread the tape through the inner rim

on the other side and pull it taut across the foam. Leaving approximately 4 in (10 cm) to spare at either end, cut the tape at both ends, unthread the needle, and fold the tape ends back tightly on to themselves so that it is all securely fixed.

(LARGER BASKETS will require further bands of adhesive tape to hold the foam securely in place.)

Cover the dry foam with a thin layer of moss, including any gaps round the edge of the basket.

For a RELATIVELY SHORT-TERM FIXING, you can use adhesive clay to stick florists' spikes on the bottom of the basket and then impale the bottom layer of foam on the spikes; tie the top, mounded, layer of foam to the bottom layer with adhesive tape.

BOWLS

EQUIPMENT
Dry foam – 1 block; florists' spike – 1; adhesive clay; sharp knife.

METHOD
Shape a dry-foam block into a mound which will fit the curve of the bowl. Using adhesive clay, stick a florists' spike firmly to the centre of the bowl. Impale the curved foam upon it, leaving the flat side up.

GLASS CONTAINERS

INGREDIENTS
Pot pourri, flat moss or paper confetti, etc. – as desired.

Dry foam – 1 or more blocks; florists' spikes – 2 or more; adhesive clay; stub/florists' wire – 2 pieces heavy gauge; sharp knife.

METHOD
Cut the dry foam to the shape of the container leaving a gap of $1/2$ in (12 mm) between the foam and the glass. (For a circular container, cut the foam into 2 mounds and tape the two pieces of foam together, flat bottom to flat bottom.)

Stick 2 or more florists' spikes to the bottom of the container with adhesive clay and impale the foam firmly on top.

Fill the gap between the foam and the container with moss, pot pourri or similar, using the stub/florists' wire as prongs to ease it down until the foam is concealed all round.

SPHERICAL VASES

EQUIPMENT
Length of 12 in (30 cm)-wide fine-gauge chicken wire; wire-cutters.

METHOD
Stretch a loose ball of chicken wire inside the container until it grips the interior surfaces.

MAKING SPHERES

SMALL FOAM SPHERE

EQUIPMENT
Dry foam – 1 block; sharp knife.

METHOD
Cut a cube from a dry-foam block. Then pare off the corners of the cube with curving cuts. Delicately cut away any edges and continue cutting off fine slivers of foam until you have a sphere.

MOSS-COVERED SPHERE

INGREDIENTS
Ordinary green 'sack' moss (*Mnium*) or sphagnum moss – 1 large packet.

EQUIPMENT
Dry foam – 1 or more blocks; length of 12 in (30 cm)-wide fine-gauge chicken wire; stub/florists' wire – 1 packet medium gauge; wire-cutters; sharp knife.

METHOD
From the roll of chicken wire cut a length which is a little longer than the desired circumference of the sphere.

In the centre of the chicken wire, make a mound of small foam cubes. Holding the mound with one hand, lift a serrated edge of the mesh with the other and fold it over the top of the mound.

Holding the first wire edge in place over the mound, lift and gently fold in the remaining edges, adding more foam cubes to fill out the sphere where necessary.

Mould the mesh and foam to get rid of uneven or flat areas, and turn any sharp wire ends inwards. Do not worry if the sphere is not perfectly round as the moss will disguise this.

Apply patches of moss and fix them in place with U-shaped pieces of stub/florists' wire until the whole sphere is thickly and firmly covered.

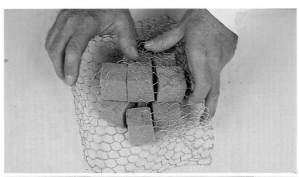

MAKING BASES FOR CIRCLES, GARLANDS OR WREATHS

SIMPLE MOSS BASE

INGREDIENTS
Damp ordinary green 'sack' moss (*Mnium*) or sphagnum moss – approx. 2 large packets.

EQUIPMENT
Circular wire wreath frame (from florist); ball of string (reel wire may be used if preferred); scissors.

METHOD
Tie the end of a reel of string to the top of the wreath frame, leaving a longish loose end beyond the knot for later.

Pick up a good handful of damp moss and hold it against the side of the frame. Bind the moss firmly in place by winding the ball of string repeatedly round the moss and frame. Bind on further handfuls of moss, overlapping one clump with another, both inside and out, all around the frame until the moss is about 1 in (2.5 cm) thick all over and evenly distributed.

When you reach the starting point, overlap the last clump of moss and tie off the binding string to the loose end of the original starting knot.

MOSS AND CHICKEN WIRE BASE

INGREDIENTS
Damp ordinary green 'sack' moss (*Mnium*) or sphagnum moss – 1 or more large packets, depending on the size of the base you require.

EQUIPMENT
12 in (30 cm)-wide fine-gauge chicken wire; reel wire; wire-cutters.

METHOD
Cut the chicken wire to the length of the circumference of the base you want.

Lay the chicken wire flat and arrange damp moss thickly and evenly along one smooth edge. Roll the mesh tightly over the moss to form a solid tube approximately 1½ in (3.5 cm) thick (or to whatever thickness you require for a particular arrangement) – tuck in stray pieces of moss and turn in any sharp spikes of wire as you roll.

Gradually bend the tube round into an even circle until the ends touch.

Attach reel wire to one end of the mesh, leaving a loose end beyond the knot for finishing. 'Sew' the two ends of the tube together with the reel wire, tie off the reel wire to the loose knot end, and tuck both reel wire ends tidily back into the green 'sack' moss.

MAKING A STEM OR BRANCH CIRCLE

The thin branches of some trees (e.g. silver birch) and shrubs, and the stems of various climbing plants (e.g. *Actinidia* vine) can be used to make circle bases. The branches or stems must be fresh and supple, and cut with secateurs into wands approximately 4½ ft (1.3m) long.

INGREDIENTS
4½ ft (1.3m) wands – approx. 7.

EQUIPMENT
Brown reel wire; wire-cutters.

METHOD
Using 1 wand, make a circle the size you require and secure it firmly with reel wire.

Take a second wand, tie one end with reel wire near where the first wand was secured, twine the second wand loosely round the first, and then tie off the second wand's end.

Plait in the rest of the wands one by one, starting and finishing each of them where appropriate to create an even thickness.

Once the circle is self-supporting, cut off the reel wire and leave the circle to dry flat in a cool place for several weeks.

WIRING

WIRING A ROSE HEAD

EQUIPMENT
Stub/florists' wire – 1 long piece of medium or fine gauge; pliers; scissors.

METHOD
Trim the stalk to approximately ¾ in (2 cm) below the rose head.

Using a pair of pliers, bend one end of the stub/florists' wire into a tiny loop.

Feed the unlooped end of the wire diagonally through the top of the flower into its base until the loop is stopped by the base. Delicately straighten the rose head on the wire.

If the wire 'stem' is going to be visible, conceal it with gutta-percha (see p.19).

WIRING A HELICHRYSUM HEAD

EQUIPMENT
Stub/florists' wire – 1 long piece medium gauge; reel of fine rose wire (in a cup to prevent it unravelling); reel of gutta-percha tape; scissors.

METHOD
Cut off the flower head leaving a stalk approximately 1½ in (3.5 cm) long.

Hold the stub/florists' wire against the stem so that one end touches the base of the flower head.

Unravel some rose wire from the reel, hold it about 2 in (5 cm) from the end in the same hand

as the stalk and stub/florists' wire. Then, with your free hand, tightly wind the rose wire round and round up towards the flower head, and back down again towards the loose end of the wire. Make sure that the end of the stalk is covered by the rose wire.

Trim the ends of the rose wire and tuck them up under the binding wire. Cover the wire 'stem' with gutta-percha tape (see below).

WIRING A FIR CONE

EQUIPMENT
Stub/florists' wire – a long piece of heavy or medium gauge, depending on the weight of the cone; reel of gutta-percha tape; pliers; wire-cutters; scissors.

METHOD
Push one end of the wire through the lowest band of scales until 2 in (5 cm) or more of it sticks out. Wind the long wire tightly round the cone inside the scales. With the pliers twist the 2 wire ends together to grip the cone.

Bend the twisted ends under the cone so that the long wire forms a 'stem'. Trim the shorter end neatly and bind two-thirds or all the wire 'stem' with brown gutta-percha tape (see below).

CONCEALING A WIRE 'STEM'

EQUIPMENT
Wired plant head; reel of adhesive gutta-percha tape – whatever colour will be least visible or most natural in the final arrangement; scissors.

METHOD
Holding the wired plant with the head upside-down and towards you, place the end of the gutta-percha tape behind the wire 'stem', close to the base of the head, at an angle of 45°.

Fold in the end corner of tape and then, keeping the tape taut, twist the wire stem so that the tape spirals up the wire just overlapping itself.

Continue to at least beyond the rose wire (if any) – cover two-thirds of the wire stem if you wish. Cut the tape and seal its end.

WIRING BUNCHES

EQUIPMENT
Stub/florists' wire – 1 long piece medium gauge; scissors.

METHOD
Most bunches are GRADED, which means that the tops of the plant heads are not all at the same height – to create a more natural appearance. A bunch that is completely flat on top would look very strange and awkward.

Remove the leaves from the stalks if you do not need them in your planned arrangement and gather a graded bunch, adjusting the heights of the heads. Trim the stalks to the desired length.

Hold one end of the stub/florists' wire level with the stalk ends so that the wire lies parallel to the stalks. About 2 in (5 cm) or more up the stalks – not too close to the plant heads, or the bunch will look stiff – bend the long wire behind the stalks and wind it diagonally round and back down over the short wire and the stalks. The remaining long end of wire forms a 'stem'.

For LOOSER GRADED BUNCHES OR SMALL CLUSTERS, after the stalks have been trimmed, place one end of the stub/florists' wire diagonally across the stalks – not too close to the heads – and wind it diagonally down the stalks. As before, leave the long wire extension as a 'stem'.

WIRING A HEAVY HEAD

EQUIPMENT
Piece of cane; stub/florists' wire – 1 long piece medium gauge; reel of gutta-percha tape; wire-cutters; scissors.

METHOD
To lengthen or strengthen a heavy-headed flower stem (e.g. globe artichoke or lotus) or a large cone, trim the plant stalk as desired leaving, if possible, a minimum of about 2½ in (7 cm), and place a piece of cane against it with one end just below the base of the plant head.

About 3 in (7.5 cm) from one end of the stub/florists' wire, bend the wire at right angles; place the shorter length parallel along the cane and stalk, and about ½ in (14mm) below the top of the cane start winding the long wire diagonally back down round the short wire, cane and stalk.

Stop wiring below the end of the stalk and trim the wire end neatly.

Bind the new 'stem' with gutta-percha of an appropriate colour (see p. 19). If the top of the cane is still visible beneath the plant head, cut it off at an angle.

LENGTHENING STEMS OR STALKS
For a stouter method see above.

EQUIPMENT
Stub/florists' wire – 1 long piece medium or heavy gauge; reel of gutta-percha tape; scissors.

METHOD
Choose a gauge of wire that will fit tightly inside the hollow stem. Insert one end of the wire 2–3 in (5–7.5 cm) inside the stem.

Cover the whole length of the stem and the wire extension with gutta-percha (see p. 19) of an appropriate colour.

ROPES, SWAGS AND FESTOONS

PLAITING A RAFFIA ROPE
Tie a bunch of raffia strands, as thick as the required rope, to a firm support like a metal bar or ring.

Divide the raffia into three equal sections, and weave the left and right sections alternately over the centre section. Keep the strands taut and proceed to the end of the plait.

Tie the end with a piece of raffia or fine rose wire and trim.

RAFFIA ROPE OF PLANTS

INGREDIENTS
A variety of flowers, grasses, ferns, etc. for bunches.

EQUIPMENT
Shanks of raffia; stub/florists' wire – medium gauge; wire-cutters; scissors.

METHOD
Plait a thick raffia rope (see above) to the desired thickness and length, and bind the ends neatly with raffia so that the rope will not fray.

Make up a small, compact bunch of flowers, grasses, etc., and wire it with stub/florists' wire (see p. 19), leaving a wire 'stem' of about 4 in (10 cm).

Insert the wire 'stem' into the thickness of the

plait near one end, with the head of the bunch towards the plait end. Bend the wire 'stem' back into the plait to secure the bunch safely. Proceed in the same way along the whole of the rope if it is to hang vertically.

HORIZONTAL RAFFIA ROPE SWAG/ FESTOON

The ingredients and equipment needed are as above.

Remember that the swag or festoon will hang in one or more loops, and allow for this when deciding the length of the raffia rope.

Basically the method is as above, except that you should mark the centre of the rope before beginning to insert the bunches at one end.

Once the centre is reached, either make up a specially designed symmetrical central bunch which emphasizes this mid-way point, or simply turn the heads of the bunches towards the other end.

NYLON ROPE SWAG/FESTOON

INGREDIENTS
A variety of flowers, grasses, ferns, etc., for bunches.
Ordinary green 'sack' moss (*Mnium*) or sphagnum moss – sufficient to cover the rope.

EQUIPMENT
$1/2$ in (1.2 cm) nylon rope – sufficient length for the swag/festoon; reel wire; stub/florists' wire – 1 or more packets medium-gauge; wire-cutters; scissors.

METHOD
Seal the ends of the nylon rope by very carefully holding it near a flame, so that the nylon melts but the rope does not catch fire.

To make a loop from which to hang the finished swag/festoon, thread the loose end of the reel wire through one end of the nylon rope and pull it through far enough for you to tie it into a loop. Do not cut off the reel of wire.

Take a good handful of moss and bind it firmly to the rope by spiralling the reel wire continuously round the moss and rope. Cover the whole length in a thick layer of moss.

Make a second hanging loop at the other end of the rope, tie off and cut the reel wire.

Flowers and other dried plant material can then be inserted into the moss rope either individually or in wired bunches (see p. 19). Only one side of the rope need be covered with flowers, etc., unless it is hanging in mid air.

Hang the completed swag/festoon round a doorway, a column, a staircase handrail, over a picture frame or wherever, and make a final check that the plant material is evenly spread.

REEL WIRE SWAG/FESTOON

INGREDIENTS
A variety of flowers, grasses, etc., sufficient for the desired length.

EQUIPMENT
Reel wire; wire-cutters; scissors.

METHOD
Unroll more than sufficient reel wire for the length of the swag/festoon you require. Tie a loop in the wire at this point, but do not cut the wire because you need it to attach the first and subsequent bunches. The loop is used to hang one end of the swag/festoon when it is complete.

Make up your first small graded bunch of dried plant material and place the bunch on top of the wire loop to conceal it. With one hand hold the stalks of the bunch against the long loose wire which will form the basis of the swag/festoon and, with the other hand, bind the bunch to that wire using the reel of wire. Pass the reel under and through the last loop of binding to make a knot and pull it tight.

Hold the second bunch so that it covers the stalks of the first bunch, bind the stalks again to the wire length with the reel of wire and tie it off as before.

Continue this process until the swag/festoon is complete and, behind the stalks of the final bunch, tie a second loop of wire with which to hang this end.

INGREDIENTS
Crimson botao/common camomile (Anthemis nobilis) – 4–5 bunches
Pink-dyed reindeer moss (Cladonia rangiferina) – 2 large packets
Pink botao/common camomile (Anthemis nobilis) – 3 bunches
Opium poppy seedheads (Papaver somniferum) – approx. 40 heads
Bearded wheat (Triticum) – 3 bunches
Wheat (Triticum) stalks – 3 bunches
Fresh ivy (Hedera sp) – several long strands

EQUIPMENT
Rustic circular basket approx. 10–12 in (25–30 cm) diameter; dry foam – 2 blocks; adhesive tape; stub/florists' wire – 1 packet medium gauge; gutta-percha tape; scissors; wire-cutters; knife.

METHOD
Shape the dry foam into a mound and tape it firmly to the centre of the base of the basket by adapting the method given on p. 15.

From the crimson botao/camomile make approximately 9 small, graded, loosely wired bunches, leaving about 6 in (15 cm) wire 'stems' (see pp. 19–20). Check that the overall length is adequate by holding the head of the first wired bunch on the rim of the basket with the wire 'stem' in or on the foam – for stability, at least 3 in (7.5 cm) of wire should penetrate the foam.

Insert the crimson clusters, some peeping over the rim, some further in, and one just off centre. Make sure that they are randomly spread.

Wire up globular clumps of reindeer moss (as for bunches, see p. 19) and insert them in the same way as the crimson botao/camomile clusters.

From the pink botao/camomile make 5 graded, not too tightly wired bunches as you did for the crimson clusters and distribute them round the basket.

Keep turning the basket to check that the bunches are naturally scattered.

Trim the stalks of the poppy seedheads to approximately 4 in (10 cm) and insert a piece of stub/florists' wire into each of them (see p. 20), binding the joint with gutta-percha tape. Insert them next to each other in groups.

Trim the wheat into short, graded clusters (see p. 19) of 3 or 5 heads, keeping a number of heads aside for later. Wire the latter too with wire 'stems'.

Insert the wheat clusters around the middle of the arrangement, but avoid placing them all in a tidy circle.

Make the wheat stalks into about 9 or more wired clusters (see p. 19), with the wire at the end of the stalks so that they splay out. Insert them around and amongst the wheat heads.

Where there are gaps, fill these with the extra wheat heads or with extra wired clumps of moss.

The final touch is added by twining ivy round the basket and the handle.

PRACTICAL HINT
Because the ingredients are wired, this arrangement can easily be adapted throughout the year by substituting different coloured plants, e.g. yellow moss plus orange and yellow miniature chrysanthemums, or a blue theme.

All the zing of spring is apparent in this crisp, luminous arrangement which would make even a lamb jump for joy.

INGREDIENTS

White baby's breath (Gypsophila sp) – 1 bunch
White sea lavender (Limonium sp) – 2 varieties,
*   2–3 bunches*
Artificial green beech (Fagus sylvatica) – 7 small
*   leafy twigs*
Mauve statice (Limonium sinuatum) – 1 bunch
Purple statice (Limonium sinuatum) – 1 bunch
White statice (Limonium sinuatum) – 1/2 bunch
Pink delphinium (Delphinium sp) – 1 bunch
Pink larkspur (Consolida sp) – 1 bunch
Orange roses – 1/2 bunch
Pink Russian/rat's tail statice (Limonium
*   suworowii) – 1 bunch*
Pink globe Amaranth (Gomphrena globosa)
*   – 4 bunches*
Grey Melaleuca (Melaleuca sp) – 2 bunches
Pink Swan River everlasting (Helipterum
*   manglesii) – 1 bunch*
White ti tree/willow myrtle (Agonis juniperina)
*   – 1/2 bunch*
White Bupleurum (Bupleurum sp) – 1/2 bunch
White delphinium (Delphinium sp) – 1 bunch
White seacrest (Helichrysum cordatum) – 1 piece
Sandplain woody pear (Xylomelum
*   angustifolium) – 2 on twig*

EQUIPMENT
Rectangular basket approx. 16 in (41 cm) × 9 in (22.5 cm); 1 ft (30 cm)-wide fine-gauge chicken wire; (optional) stub/florists' wire – 1 packet medium gauge; (optional) reel of fine rose wire; (optional) reel of gutta-percha tape; wire-cutters; scissors.

METHOD
Cut a length of chicken wire sufficient to roll into an oblong to fill the basket.

The hazy *Gypsophila* and sea lavender comprise the basis of the arrangement, so begin by inserting them – the shorter, more splayed pieces round the edge, the taller pieces towards the centre.

The green beech leaves go in next, followed by the pink delphiniums and the smaller pink larkspur.

The stalks of statice of various kinds and ▷

On a warm summer day even the prettiest room seems fresher and more inviting when it contains such a delightful arrangement.

◁ colours are then scattered round the basket.
Working from the top centre towards the rim of the basket, insert the remaining ingredients in any order you wish. There is no hard and fast rule once you have created the basic shape of this arrangement.

The rose, *Helipterum* and *Helichrysum* heads may all be wired individually, if desired (see pp. 18–19).

PRACTICAL HINT
To protect the surface of a wooden table from scratching, cover the underside of the basket with felt from a self-adhesive roll or glued on.

INGREDIENTS
Wild oats (Avena fatua) – 1 bunch
Natural bearded wheat (Triticum) or barley
(Hordeum sp) – 1 bunch
Orange six-rowed barley (Hordeum sp) – 1
bunch
White sea lavender (Limonium sp) – 2 bunches
Red broom bloom (Gypsophila rugosa) – 2
bunches
Pink delphiniums (Delphinium sp) – 1–2
bunches
Golden poppy seedheads (Papaver gigantum)
– 3 or 5 heads
Silver everlasting/strawflowers (Helichrysum
vestium) – 1 bunch
Peachy orange everlasting/strawflowers
(Helichrysum bracteatum) – 2 bunches

EQUIPMENT
Basket – approx. 12 in (30 cm) diameter; lace –
approx. 3 ft (90 cm) long; coarse needle and
thread; dry foam – 2 blocks; adhesive tape; stub/
florists' wire – 1 packet medium gauge; reel of
fine rose wire; reel of beige or brown gutta-
percha tape; scissors; wire-cutters; knife.

METHOD
With a needle and thread, loosely gather the lace
and sew it to the inside of the basket so that it
forms a ruff around the edge.

Carve the dry foam into a dome shape to fill
the container and fix it in place with adhesive
tape (see p. 15).

To create the outline of the arrangement, place
the oats and bearded wheat or barley around the
basket, turning it as you do so. Trim the stems, if
necessary, so that the heads are about the same
height as the basket handle or about 1½ times
the height of the container.

Insert the sea lavender at irregular points all
over the basket, wiring it into bunches (see p. 19)
if the stems are short. This will form the base of
the arrangement.

Next comes the red broom bloom, divided into
approximately 11 clusters, wired to leave a 4 in
(10 cm) wire 'stem', and spaced irregularly round
the basket to about the same height as the ▷

Autumn, season of mists and mellow fruitfulness, reflected in romantic shades of gold, red, peach, pink and white with a touch of lace.

◁ bottom of the oat and barley heads.

Check that no dry foam is visible. If it is, cover it with further sea lavender or broom bloom.

Now add the delphiniums and poppy heads.

Wire the heads of *Helichrysum* and bind the wire 'stems' with gutta-percha tape (see pp. 18–19). Very delicately place some around the edge, peeping over the lace, and others just above the broom bloom and sea lavender in the centre.

Finally double check that no foam is visible and that the arrangement looks natural from every angle.

INGREDIENTS
Electric or battery-powered candles – 2 or more
Larch (Larix sp) – large bunch of branches with
  cones
Fir cones – 9 or more large ones
Sphagnum moss – 1 packet

EQUIPMENT
Terracotta clay pot or container – large; dry foam – 2 or more blocks; adhesive tape; stub/florists' wire – 1 packet medium gauge; gutta-percha tape; wire-cutters; knife.

METHOD
If you gather the larch branches yourself, make sure you cut them cleanly with sharp secateurs to avoid damaging the tree.

Shape the dry foam to fit the container snugly, otherwise you will have to tape or wire it into the pot or basket.

Tape the candles firmly in place on the foam. Insert the first few larch branches in the middle of the foam block furthest from you and then work towards the sides and back edge. Make sure the branches enter the foam at an angle so that they look as natural as possible.

Wire the large fir cones – some the right way up and others upside-down – with stub/florists' wire (see p. 19), leaving 7 in (17.5 cm) or more as a stem. Place them around the edge of the container, some drooping over the rim. Insert some higher up, off centre, so that the arrangement does not look too symmetrical.

Now add a few small larch branches so that they fall over the cones. Check that there are no bare gaps where the foam is visible; if it is and there is not enough space to insert another cone, push in a small clump of sphagnum moss fixed with U-shaped stub/florists' wire.

PRACTICAL HINT
Never use lighted wax candles amongst dried material – it is extremely dangerous.

To make this arrangement look more festive, add gold- or silver-sprayed branches, orange Chinese lanterns/bladder cherry (*Physalis alkekengi franchetii*) or some scarlet celosia cockscomb (*Celosia argentea cristata*).

Winter – candles glimmer amongst larch in this simple yet effective arrangement,

which looks particularly well in a hall or living room corner.

Ingredients
Wheat – 9–10 bunches
Fungi – 8 or more large pieces
Hair grass (Aira sp) or raffia – 1 bunch

Equipment
Terracotta clay pot or container – approx. 12 in (30 cm) diameter; length of coarse-gauge chicken wire; stub/florists' wire – 4 packets coarse gauge; black or brown reel wire; wire-cutters; knife.

Method
Bend the chicken wire into a rough ball to fit the container and press it flat on top.

Gather bunches of wheat small enough for the stems to go through the holes of the chicken wire and bind them with stub/florists' wire about one third of the way up the stems so that the bunches are compact and upright. Place the first few bunches vertically in the centre, but do not worry if they lean outwards slightly as they near the rim. Pack them in fairly closely. Raise some and lower others so that the overall effect is that of a randomly gathered sheaf.

Wrap reel wire round the fungi stems and, if you can, attach them to the chicken wire at varying angles round the edge of the pot so that they conceal the wire round the wheat bunches. The fungi should overlap, thus also hiding the chicken wire. Check all round the container.

To make the bow, on a flat surface fold the grass or raffia into a bow shape (no need to tie a real one) and fix it in place in the centre with whichever material you are using or a bit of fine wire. (If you can persuade a friend to help you do this, so much the easier, as it is a task which ideally needs three hands!) If stray ends spring out around the bow, do not worry – it will look softer. Bind the ends with grass or raffia by using 3 or 4 strands of grass or 1 of raffia. Place one end of the binding material level with the end of the bow, run the binding 'string' up the bow for about 2 in (5 cm) and then bind round and down towards the bottom over your first loose end. When you reach the bottom, trim the binding material and glue it firmly in place. You can, if you prefer, leave the ends of the bow unbound.

Harvest Thanksgiving – a striking combination of wheat, apples, gourds, nuts,

fir cones and fungi provide an appropriate tribute to nature's abundance.

PAIR OF WHEAT POTS

INGREDIENTS
Wheat (Triticum) – 2 bunches
Sphagnum moss – 1 small packet

EQUIPMENT
4 terracotta clay pots (2 to fill, 2 to stand them on) – approx. 6 in (15 cm) high; dry foam – 2 blocks; stub/florists' wire – 1 packet medium gauge; beige and green raffia; florists' spikes – 2; adhesive clay; wire-cutters; knife; scissors.

METHOD
Sculpt the dry foam to fill both pots to within 1 in (2.5 cm) of the rims. Fix the foam in place by impaling it upon a florists' spike stuck to the bottom of each pot with adhesive clay.

For the first pot, take a good handful of wheat and tie it with wire about 1 in (2.5 cm) below the heads. Add another thick layer of wheat all round this core and tie it firmly with a length of twisted or plaited raffia. Also tie the bunch with wire about 4 in (10 cm) from the end of the stalks. Press the base of the bunch firmly into the dry foam and cover the top of the pot and the wiring on the bunch with moss affixed by U-shaped pieces of stub/florists' wire.

The second pot is handled in the same way.

MANTELPIECE

INGREDIENTS
Larch branches (Larix sp), some with cones – 6
Artichokes (Cynara scolymus) – 10
Golden yarrow (Achillea filipendulina) – 7 pieces
Golden lady's mantle (Alchemilla mollis) – 3 bunches
Red everlasting/strawflowers (Helichrysum bracteatum) – 3 bunches

Mexican white pine cones – 9 or more
Wheat (Triticum) – 3 bunches
Ivy (Hedera sp) – 1 bunch
Sparkly gauze ribbon or coarse hessian
Matt gold baubles – about 12

EQUIPMENT
Dry foam – approx. 5 plus ½ block beneath each end; adhesive tape; stub/florists' wire – 2 packets medium gauge; scissors; knife.

METHOD
Place the dry-foam blocks end to end along the mantelpiece and tape them to each other and then to the mantelpiece. Attach half a block with tape beneath each end of the mantelpiece.

Insert pieces of larch all along the foam.

Attach a length of stub/florists' wire to the individual artichokes as you would when wiring a bunch (see p. 19) and insert them in 2 groups, 1 left of centre, the other to the right.

Add the golden yarrow piece by piece.

Wire the 3 bunches of *Alchemilla* and the 3 bunches of *Helichrysum*. Place 1 bunch of *Alchemilla* by the right-hand pot, 1 right of centre and 1 towards the left, at the back. Place 2 bunches of red *Helichrysum* right of centre and 1 bunch left of centre.

Wire the pine cones (see p. 19) and insert them at intervals among the rest of the ingredients.

Make the wheat into 4 loose, fan-shaped bunches tied with wire in the middle, with some pieces of wheat top to toe. Include spare wheat stalks if you have them and insert these bunches at either end and on the front.

Twine lengths of ivy in and around the mantelpiece, fixing it where necessary to the foam by U-shaped pieces of stub/florists' wire.

Tie the hessian/ribbon into 4 bows and place them, together with the golden baubles, using U-shaped pieces of wire to attach them.

Tired holly and tacky tinsel are definitely surplus to requirements when a fireplace is transformed by this spectacular, natural-looking arrangement.

INGREDIENTS

Fungi – 4, medium flat

Opium poppy seedheads (Papaver somniferum)
  – 16, medium

Protea compacta flat – 2

Green, red and natural brown seedpod heads –
  9 any variety

Lotus flower (fruit) (Nelumbo lucifera) – 4

Golden mushrooms – 4

Scots pine cones (Pinus sylvestris) – 3, medium

Larch cones (Larix sp) – 13

Miniature rattan palm/wait-a-while vine
  (Calamus sp) – 1 branch with cones

'Mercedes' red hybrid tea roses – 1 bunch (18
  heads)

Lavender (Lavendula spica) – 2 bunches

Bleached wheat (Triticum) – 1 bunch

White small-flowered delphinium (Delphinium
  sp) – 3 heads

Pink peppercorns on stems – 1 packet (6 clusters)

Ordinary green 'sack' moss (Mnium) – 2 packets

Bun moss (Grimmia pulvinata) – 1 packet

Nuts – 2 large bags any edible variety

Artificial ivy (Hedera sp) – 4 short pieces

EQUIPMENT

2-tier circular basket: lower 18 in (45 cm) diameter, 3½ in (8.5 cm) deep; upper 9 in (22.5 cm) diameter, 2½ in (6.5 cm) deep; church candles – 3; dry foam – 2 blocks; stub/florists' wire – 1 packet medium gauge, 1 packet fine gauge; cold glue; adhesive tape; wire-cutters; scissors; knife.

METHOD

Fill the gap beneath the upper tier of the basket with ordinary moss.

Cut the dry foam into 4 cubes each 3 in (7.5 cm) square and attach them with adhesive tape to the base of the lower tier at the 4 points of the compass: north, south, east and west.

Wrap one end of a piece of medium-gauge wire round the stalks of the fungi as for a bunch (see p. 19) and insert their wire 'stems' in the foam, 1 in each block, so that they project beyond the basket rim or to the side of the dry foam.

Trim the stalks of the poppies, *Protea*, seed heads, lotus and golden mushrooms as necessary, and distribute them amongst the 4 foam blocks.

Wire up the 3 Scots pine cones and about 7 of the small larch cones (see p. 19), and share them between the blocks.

Divide the branch of *Calamus* cones into 4, wind a piece of medium-gauge wire round each (see pp. 19–20) and insert 1 cluster in each block.

Trim the rose stalks to about 3 in (7.5 cm) and distribute 8 of them around the blocks. (Wire the individual heads first, as on p. 18, if the stalks are too fragile.)

Make the lavender into 10 graded, wired clusters (see pp. 19–20) and the wheat into 8 similar clusters. Disperse them over the blocks.

The 3 white delphinium heads are each divided into 4 pieces, wired as you would a bunch (see p. 19) and 3 clusters are inserted in each block.

Half the pink peppercorns on stalks are attached in clusters to each foam block using U-shaped pieces of stub/florists' wire.

Attach the candles to the base of the top tier of the basket with adhesive tape and pack ordinary moss tightly around them. Cover this with green bun moss affixed by U-shaped pieces of wire.

Decorate the rim of the top tier with the remaining roses (push the stalks into the moss), cones (wired, as above, or glued on) and clusters of peppercorns (attached by U-shaped pieces of wire).

Finally, fill the 4 empty quarters of the lower tier with nuts, scatter a few over the bun moss and attach the ivy with 'hairpins' of wire to the rim of the basket or where you will.

PRACTICAL HINT

Instead of purchasing a 2-tier basket, use 2 separate baskets of appropriate dimensions. Trim the corners off a foam block so that they will not protrude beyond the edge of the smaller basket and fix the foam to the centre of the large basket with adhesive tape. Then fix the small basket firmly on top of the foam with U-shaped pieces of stub/florists' wire pushed through the base of the basket.

As a variation, you could replace the nuts with prettily wrapped chocolates.

JULIET WILLIS

The wide variety of attractive ingredients in this unusual two-tier basket are a source of endless fascination long after the festive season is over.

INGREDIENTS
Opium poppy seedheads (Papaver somniferum)
  – 15 or more
Lotus flower (fruit) (Nelumbo lucifera) – 3 large,
  8 medium
Scots pine cones (Pinus sylvestris) – 6 or more
Larch cones (Larix sp) – 11 or more
Eucalyptus baby (Eucalyptus sp) – 1–2 bunches
Palm spears (Palmatus sp) – 8 various sizes
White safflower (Carthamus sp) – 3 bunches
Matt bronze Christmas baubles – 5 or more

EQUIPMENT
Vine ring base (from florist); brown reel wire; gold paint – 1 small tin; small paint brush; glue gun (preferably) or cold glue; wire-cutters; scissors.

METHOD
Paint gold on the tips of some of the poppy seedheads, some of the lotus heads and, if you wish, some of the cones. Brush the gold on lightly rather than painting solidly.

Begin by attaching the pointed palm spears to the back of the base with reel wire so that they create a strong outline.

The blue-tinged eucalyptus in clusters of varying lengths is tied all round the side of the base. Wind one end of the reel wire round the eucalyptus stalks as you would a bunch of flowers (see p. 19), wind the reel of wire round the base, cut it and tie the loose end firmly to the wired bunch so that the cluster stays firmly in place.

Wire the 6 Scots pine cones with reel wire (see p. 19) and tie them to the garland at intervals, some on the inner edge, some on the outer edge and 1 or more in the middle.

Next with reel wire, make up as many mixed wired bunches (see p. 19) as you can, using white safflowers (trimmed to 3 in/7.5 cm), lotus heads and poppy seedheads. Tie these to the frame in the same way as the eucalyptus.

To cover any remaining obvious gaps and to make the garland look uncontrived, either glue the small larch cones (singly or in groups) straight on to the base or attach a length of reel wire to the bottom of each with a blob of glue and, when the glue is dry, tie them to the frame. The former method is quicker and less fiddly.

Finally attach the matt bronze baubles either with glue or reel wire.

PRACTICAL HINT
This particular garland is very adaptable. For a change of festive colour scheme spray some of the ingredients with any shade of metallic car spray paint (sold in cans at garages or DIY shops) and add baubles or small bows of your choice.

To use indoors in the summer the whole garland can be spray-painted white, for instance, with a little silver or gold.

JULIET WILLIS

A joy for Christmas, the strong shapes used in this garland also look stunning

when sprayed different hues to suit other seasons or occasions.

INGREDIENTS

Straight tree branches – 1 × 1 in (2.5 cm)
  diameter, 3 ft 6 in (1.05 m) long; 8 × ¹/₂ in
  (1.3 cm) diameter, 27 in (67.5 cm) long
Pliable vines – 15 or more, some ¹/₂ in (1.3 cm)
  diameter, some thinner
Larch cones (Larix sp) – 80
Scots pine cones (Pinus sylvestris) – 19
Walnuts – 18
Small dark red chrysanthemums
  (Chrysanthemum sp) – 30
Green ivy leaves (Hedera sp) – 27
Red chilli peppers – 27
Cinnamon sticks – 16
Bearded wheat (Triticum sp) – 6 pieces
Chinese lantern/bladder cherry (Physalis
  alkekengi franchetii) – 30 heads
Flat moss (Mnium sp) – 1 square

EQUIPMENT

Terracotta clay pot – approx. 8 in (20 cm) diameter; 1 packet plaster of Paris and 1 block of dry foam or 1 packet of quick-drying cement; mixing bowl and stirring implement; glue gun; reel of green or brown rose wire, or very fine green or brown reel wire; ordinary brown reel wire; beige raffia; wire-cutters; scissors; knife.

METHOD

Line the pot with slices of dry foam, if you are using plaster, to prevent the pot cracking.

Make a thick, creamy mix of plaster or cement and fill over three-quarters of the pot. Quickly rinse the mixing bowl and stirrer, and whizz back to the pot.

Insert the tree trunk in the pot and turn it several times so that it is well coated by the mixture. Tap the base of the pot a couple of times to ensure the mix has settled. Hold or prop up the trunk vertically until the base has set hard.

Whilst the vines are still pliable, loosely plait 3 of the thickest into a circle approximately 1 ft 6 in (45 cm) in diameter and tie it in place with coarser reel wire (see p. 18).

Push the ends of the 8 straight branches into the circle at even intervals and tie them all loosely at the top with coarser reel wire so that they form a teepee shape.

Weave the remaining vines in and around, up and down the 'teepee' and across the base circle. Tie them, where necessary, with fine reel wire.

Lift the 'teepee' on to the tree trunk and tie it tightly to the top with the reel wire that is already loosely holding the top of the 'teepee' together. Also glue the junction to make sure it holds firm.

Cut 20 6-in (15-cm) lengths of fine reel or rose wire and glue the bases of 4 larch cones along the middle section of each piece of wire. When the cones are firmly fixed, tie the wires to the tree at irregular intervals so that the cones form square rosettes.

Wire the Scots pine cones (see p. 19) either with ordinary or fine reel wire and attach them to the tree randomly.

Glue the walnuts and red chrysanthemum heads on to the tree in threes.

Glue on the ivy leaves in groups of 3 and on top of them glue 3 chilli peppers in a fan shape.

Cut the cinnamon sticks in half (unless they are longer than usual, in which case cut them into 3). Make them into 8 bundles of 4 tied neatly with a thin piece of raffia. Glue them around the tree at various angles.

Use several wheat heads glued round the tip of the tree to hide the wiring and insert 3 heads so that they stand up on top – glue them in place, if necessary.

Glue the *Physalis* heads to the centre of some of the clusters of larch cones and walnuts, or wherever you think they look most effective.

Glue on pieces of flat moss to cover the base.

Who needs the hassle of fusing fairy lights and shedding pine needles when dried

flowers and plants can create such a decorative and original tree?

INGREDIENTS
Ordinary green 'sack' moss (Mnium) – 1 large packet
Artificial green leaves – 3
Artificial fruit – 5 clusters of blackberries, 2 red apples, 2 clusters black grapes, 1 pear, 1 red pomegranate, 2 clusters of cranberries, 2 clusters of crab apples
Larch cones (Larix sp) – 13

EQUIPMENT
Terracotta clay pots – 1 × 7 in (17.5 cm) diameter, 1 × 4 in (10 cm) diameter; church candle; 'dry hard' clay; adhesive tape; stub/florists' wire – 1 packet medium gauge, 1 packet fine gauge; wire-cutters; scissors.

METHOD
Pack the bottom of the large terracotta clay pot with moss to provide a steady base for the small pot.

Stand the small pot in the centre of the large one so that the top of the former stands out about 3 in (7.5 cm) above the rim of the latter. Pack more moss firmly round the small pot.

To ensure that the candle will not wobble, stick it securely to the base of the small pot with 'dry hard' clay and adhesive tape. When the clay has hardened, surround it with moss pressed in with your fingertips.

Attach a piece of medium-gauge stub/florists' wire to each of the green leaves as you would to a bunch of flowers (see pp. 19–20) and insert the wire 'stems' deep into the large pot, curving them so that the leaves hang well below the rim.

Bend one end of a piece of medium-gauge wire into a triangle and, holding the long wire 'stem' towards you, stick the flat 'base' of the wire triangle with adhesive tape on to the base of the pear. Bend the wire 'stem' into a curve so that it will hold the pear in place when inserted all the way into the moss in the large pot.

Do the same for the 2 red apples and for the pomegranate, but attach the wire 'stem' to the top of the latter, where the stalk would be, so that its attractive base is visible.

Using pieces of medium-gauge stub/florists' wire, the blackberries, cranberries, black grapes, cranberries and crab apples are each given a wire 'stem' as you would for a small bunch of flowers (see pp. 19–20).

Insert the clusters of fruit round the edge of the large pot.

Finally the small larch cones are wired using fine-gauge stub/florists' wire (see p. 19) and are inserted wherever there is a gap or they look most effective.

PRACTICAL HINT
For safety, before the candle is lit, dampen the moss in the small pot if there seems any likelihood of it catching fire.

Fresh fruit could easily be substituted for the artificial, but the arrangement may then be eaten.

PARTERRE

Almost good enough to eat, this potful of fruit and cones strikes a merry note to complement the Christmas feasting.

For a party or to jazz up plain surroundings, choose an uncomplicated design in rich, exciting colours with a hint of glitter.

JULIET WILLIS

INGREDIENTS
Blue, gold, green, red, pink, silver and cognac Silver dollar gum (Eucalyptus cinerea) – 4 bunches
Mauve, orange, green and blue Hoja or other large leaves on stems – 9
Red yarrow (Achillea filipendulina) – 13 stems
Black semaphore sedge/rush (Juncus sp) – 3 bunches

EQUIPMENT
Round black or dark blue vase; coarse-gauge chicken wire; stub/florists' wire – 1 packet long, medium gauge; gold and silver spray paint (from artists' suppliers/craft shops); blue, green, red, pink, cognac, mauve and orange metallic car spray paint (from DIY shops or garages).

METHOD
Mould the chicken wire to fill the container.

On the shorter pieces of eucalyptus, wind one end of a piece of stub/florists' wire round each stalk, leaving a wire 'stem' below (see pp. 19–20). These pieces will be used round the edge of the vase, because the wire can be bent so that the eucalyptus hangs down to soften the outline.

Spray all the eucalyptus and the Hoja or other large leaves with your choice of spray paints – but do not cover too many with silver or gold since glints are more effective than a mass of sparkle, unless it is Christmas or a silver or golden wedding anniversary.

When these ingredients are dry, spread the eucalyptus round the vase and insert the large leaves in the middle to fill in the centre.

Next scatter the red *Achillea* around the vase at varying heights.

Lastly insert the delicate, spiky semaphore sedge so that it softens the outline. Extend the stems, if necessary, with stub/florists' wire (see p. 20).

PRACTICAL HINT
Try spraying one length of eucalyptus with more than one colour. You could also try spraying one side of the leaves one colour and the other side another.

INGREDIENTS
Pinky-mauve statice (Limonium sp) – 1 piece
Mauve statice (Limonium sp) – 1 bunch
*Mauve-blue delphinium (Delphinium sp) – 3
  heads*
Lavender (Lavendula spica) – 1 bunch
*Green hydrangea (Hydrangea macrophylla) – 2
  heads*
Cream nipplewort (Lapsana sp) – 1/2 bunch
Lotus flower (fruit) (Nelumbo lucifera) – 7 small
*Maroon peony buds (Paeonia lactiflora) – 6
  large, half open*

EQUIPMENT
Broad-brimmed straw hat; stub/florists' wire – 1
packet fine gauge; wire-cutters; glue gun; scissors; rose pink paper ribbon.

METHOD
Divide the mauve statice into 3, the delphinium
into 7, the lavender into 3, the hydrangea into 6,
and the nipplewort into 3.

Including blue or mauve in each, wire all the
ingredients into 14 or more small, mixed, graded,
wired bunches (see p. 19).

Glue the bunches round the crown, working
from the centre of the front towards the back,
overlapping each bunch to hide the wiring of the
previous one. The heads of the bunches all point
towards the front. Almost three-quarters of the
crown is covered in this way, leaving room for
the bow at the back.

Tie the paper ribbon into a large, generous
bow and glue it to the hat. Trim the ends of the
ribbon diagonally.

JULIET WILLIS

Hang one on the wall, lay one

on the chair or bed

in the guest room, or simply wear

one with pleasure and pride.

INGREDIENTS
*Branches or vine stems – 5 thin, flexible, approx.
15 in (37.5 cm) long*
Leaves – 26 or more, very large, any variety

EQUIPMENT
Stub/florists' wire – 1 piece medium gauge; reel of fine rose wire; cold glue or glue gun; wire-cutters; scissors.

METHOD
To form the base of the dish, bend 1 branch or vine into a circle about 6 in (15 cm) in diameter and tie it firmly with rose wire.

The basic shape of a shallow bowl is formed by wiring one end of another branch or vine to the top of the flat circle at an angle of about 30° from the horizontal, bending the wand into a loop and attaching the other end, about 2 in (5 cm) away from the first, again at an angle, to the top of the circle with wire.

Attach the other 3 wands in the same manner, so that you have 2 pairs of loops opposite each other – 1 north, 1 south; 1 east, 1 west.

Take 4 leaves and place them on the work surface with their stalk ends overlapping and with their heads pointing north, south, east and west.

Using the stub/florists' wire to make 2 holes through the centre, where the leaf bases overlap, thread a 12 in (30 cm) length of rose wire through from the front of the leaves to the back and up through the other hole. Twist the two wire ends together to make what is, in effect, a flat wire 'stitch' holding the leaves together. Trim the wire ends neatly.

Over each of the 4 gaps between the leaves glue another leaf to parts of the 2 beneath. As you do so, try to make the leaves gradually curve up from the horizontal to create a dish.

Add further leaves in the same way until the dish is the size you require.

To attach the leaves to the base, either glue the underside of the leaves to the base circle or, using the stub/florists' wire to puncture 2 circles of holes through the leaves on either side of the base circle, 'stitch' the leaves to the base with a long length of rose wire threaded continuously round the base and through the leaves.

Tie the two loose wire ends together when the circle of 'stitches' is complete.

Lastly, glue 1 large leaf in the centre of the dish to cover any wiring or ugly ends.

PRACTICAL HINT
Dried gourds or pot pourri are ideal for putting in this dish because they are light enough not to damage it.

MCQUEEN'S

There is more than a hint of South Sea island charm and hospitality in this distinctive present even when it is made from locally gathered leaves.

INGREDIENTS
Fresh bay leaves – approx. 70

EQUIPMENT
Dry-foam sphere (from florist) – approx. 7 in (17.5 cm) diameter; stub/florists' wire – 2 packets medium gauge; cold glue; large piece of muslin; wire-cutters.

METHOD
While the bay leaves are still fresh and pliable, wire them at each end into the foam using U-shaped pieces of stub/florists' wire. Place them in parallel, overlapping rows.

To cover the wires, glue on bay leaves overlapping end to end at right angles to the first layer of bay leaves.

Wrap the whole ball in muslin, tie it tightly, and leave it for 1 week – this will prevent the leaves from bending outwards.

PRACTICAL HINT
Make tennis ball-sized spheres in the same way, but fix the final end-over-end strips of bay leaves with cloves as well as glue, and hang them on the Christmas tree or present them to friends.

PARTERRE

No, they are not cabbages! One or more bay leaf balls make an unusual, witty gift or the type of stylish composition beloved by interior designers.

INGREDIENTS
Red roses – 4–6 bunches (70–80 blooms)
Sphagnum moss – 1 small packet

EQUIPMENT
Wooden box or other container – approx. 17 in (43 cm) × 12 in (30 cm) × 3½ in (9 cm); dry foam – 5–6 blocks; stub/florists' wire – 1 packet medium gauge; wire-cutters; knife; broad red paper ribbon – approx. 2 yds (1.8 m).

METHOD
Pack the dry foam into the box so that it is snugly filled. Trim the foam if necessary.

Place the roses in straight, regular lines right across the container.

If any foam is visible round the edges, tuck in small amounts of sphagnum moss fixed, if necessary, with short 'hairpins' of U-shaped stub/florists' wire.

Cut one length of ribbon and wrap it closely round the middle of the roses. Pin the two ends firmly together.

Cut a second, longer length and drape it round the back of the box, bringing the two ends to the front, where you pin them with stub/florists' wire to the cross-over in the first ribbon.

Tie a large, loose knot in the third length of ribbon. Fix it with a short U-shaped piece of stub/florists' wire through the cross-over of the wrapping ribbons, and bend the two wire ends sideways to keep the knot in place. Adjust the knot and spread the ends attractively, trimming them if necessary.

PRACTICAL HINT
You can use fewer roses in this arrangement, and thus make it more economical, by buying fully open blooms, or opening them fully yourself (see p. 52).

PARTERRE

PARTERRE

Extravagant-looking roses displayed with panache make a stunning feature

or an unforgettable present for someone special.

INGREDIENTS
Ordinary green 'sack' moss (Mnium) – 1 small packet
Red hybrid tea roses – 2 bunches, open if possible

EQUIPMENT
Heart-shaped basket approx. 7 in (17.5 cm) × 7 in; dry foam – 1 block; stub/florists' wire – 1 packet medium gauge, 1 packet fine gauge; cold glue; wire-cutters; scissors; knife.

METHOD
Shape the dry foam to fill half the depth of the basket and to fit the heart shape snugly.

Using U-shaped pieces of medium-gauge stub/florists' wire, attach small loose clumps of moss to cover the dry foam.

You can, if you wish, wire the individual rose heads with fine-gauge stub/florists' wire (see p. 18) before placing them in the basket. Otherwise, trim the rose stalks to leave about 4 in (10 cm) below the blooms and insert them directly into the dry foam.

Start by inserting the roses at the top and work downwards. Leave a slight gap between each bloom and avoid placing them in rows – they should not look too regimented.

Gaps round roses without leaves are filled either by the lazy method of simply tucking in odd leaves with your fingertips or by the more stable method of glueing the bases of the leaves singly or in pairs to a piece of fine-gauge stub/florists' wire and inching them into the foam.-

Whichever method you employ, allow some leaves to soften the outline vertically and horizontally.

PRACTICAL HINT
If the roses you have bought are closed buds, before trimming the stalks, hold each flower in the steam above a boiling kettle or pan of water until the petals unfold, but beware – this makes them even more fragile.

Always keep any surplus leaves and stalks in a cool, dry place for use in another arrangement – never throw them away.

MCQUEEN'S

Capture the heart of a loved one with an alluring basket of gorgeous roses – and then make a matching one for yourself.

PARTERRE

INGREDIENTS
Ordinary green 'sack' moss (Mnium) – 1 sack
Green bun (Grimmia pulvinata) or reindeer
*   (Cladonia rangiferina) moss – 3 large packets*
Bleached reindeer moss (Cladonia rangiferina) –
*   1 large packet*

EQUIPMENT
Metal funeral wreath frame in the shape of a
teddy bear (from florist); green reel wire; black
button eyes (from needlecraft shop) – 2; plastic
or polystyrene for teeth – 2 bits; stub/florists'
wire – 2 packets thick gauge; yellow paper ribbon; cold glue; green spray paint.

METHOD
First of all the teddy bear wreath frame has to be
bent into a shape more closely resembling a
rabbit. For instance, the bear's nose has to be
flattened somewhat and the ears extended with
chicken wire covered with moss.

   Fill the body, arms, legs and head with ordinary moss (it is cheaper than other types) and
pack it in tight. Once all these parts are plump

enough, wrap them in reel wire to keep the moss
in place.

   Tight clumps of green bun or reindeer moss
are then affixed by U-shaped pieces of stub/flor-
ists' wire or with glue. Cover the whole body
except the insides of the ears and the ends of the
paws. If necessary, spray the rabbit with green
spray paint to disguise the glue.

   Carefully attach the bleached reindeer moss to
the insides of the ears and on the paws.

   Trim any whiskery or stray ends of moss
which are sticking out since the outline of the
rabbit's coat should be quite sleek.

   Wire in the black button eyes, invent a couple
of buck teeth, and use stub/florists' wire for
whiskers. Cover the wires in gutta-percha for
safety.

   Once a large yellow paper bow has been tied
round its neck, the rabbit is ready for naming.

PRACTICAL HINT
Keep this rabbit on a high shelf, well out of reach
of small children – the eyes and whiskers can be
particularly dangerous.

PARTERRE

For Easter, Peter Rabbit has his best bow on, but he and Teddy Bear are smart,

decorative features, not cuddly toys for children.

INGREDIENTS

Wine red broom bloom (Gypsophila rugosa) – 3 bunches

Golden yarrow (Achillea filipendulina) – 6 heads

Orange-red everlasting/strawflowers (Helichrysum bracteatum) – 2 bunches

Very dark red everlasting/strawflowers (Helichrysum bracteatum) – 2 bunches

Yellow Helipterum Sandfordii – 2 bunches

Maroon peonies (Paeonia lactiflora) – 5 blooms medium to small

Green sea lavender (Limonium sp) – 1¹/₂–2 bunches

Contorted willow (Salix sp) – 5 short pieces

EQUIPMENT

Dry-foam – 1–2 blocks; rush-covered basket – approx. 12 in (30 cm) × 6 in (15 cm) × 6 in (15 cm); stub/florists' wire – 1 packet medium gauge; reel of fine rose wire; reel of adhesive tape; pliers; wire-cutters; scissors; knife.

METHOD

Shape the dry-foam blocks so that they will fill the basket and tie them firmly in place using adhesive tape (see p. 15).

Using stub/florists' wire, make up 6 compact clusters of broom bloom (see p. 19), leaving a wire 'stem' approx. 5 in (12.5 cm) long below the trimmed stalks. (The overall height of a wired cluster when it is inserted in the centre of the arrangement should be about 7 in/17.5 cm or more.) Insert the wired clusters of broom bloom starting in the middle and then work towards the edges.

Next, insert the 6 golden *Achillea* heads into the foam at various points.

Using rose wire and stub/florists' wire, wire up about 5 individual orange heads and 5 dark red heads of *Helichrysum* (see p. 18), and keep them aside for later.

Wire the rest of the *Helichrysum* straight into 5 small orange bunches and 7 small dark red bunches (see p. 19). Leave a good 5–6 in (12.5–15 cm) wire 'stem' on each bunch and place them around the basket. ▷

PARTERRE

Bold does not necessarily mean gaudy - the excitement of vibrant colours brings warmth to a neglected spot and raises one's spirits.

◁ Next insert 6 wired clusters (see p. 19) of yellow *Sandfordii* on 5–6 in (12.5–15 cm) wire 'stems'. Then position the 5 maroon peonies.

Wire about 13 clusters (see p. 19) of green sea lavender and tuck them in round the edges of the basket and into a few gaps.

The individually wired heads of *Helichrysum*, which were set aside earlier, are bent over the sides of the basket and inserted in twos and threes in any remaining gaps or where you think they will add impact.

Finally wire the ends of 5 or more pieces of contorted willow using stub/florists' wire, leaving 6 in (15 cm) wire 'stems', and place the willow so that it curls through and out beyond the flowers to break the hard outline.

INGREDIENTS
Baby's breath (Gypsophila sp) – 2 bunches
White delphinium (Delphinium sp) – 1–1¹/₂
bunches
Love-lies-bleeding (Amaranthus sp) – 1 bunch
Wheat (Triticum) – 1 bunch
Opium poppy seedheads (Papaver somniferum)
– 6 large
Honesty (Lunaria rediviva) – 1–1¹/₂ bunches
Pink sunray (Helipterum sp) – 2 bunches
White sunray (Helipterum sp) – 1 bunch

EQUIPMENT
Container – 7–8 in (17.5–20 cm) high; fine-gauge
chicken wire; wire-cutters; scissors.

METHOD
Press a 12 in (30 cm) length of chicken wire into
a roughly oval ball inside the container.

Remember that if the arrangement is on a
windowsill, it will be visible from outside as well
as inside and the dried plants must be arranged to
take this into account. Arrange it *in situ*, regularly checking from all angles.

Begin by putting in the *Gypsophila*, keeping
aside a few short pieces for use later. The spread
should be fairly even, higher at the back and
extending forwards at the front.

Remove most of the leaves from the white
delphinium and pink *Amaranthus* and place the

flowers, together with the wheat, in the middle
and towards the back to create a fan-shaped
effect. If necessary, extend the wheat stems with
wire (see p. 20).

Place the poppy heads towards the rear, punctuating the overall shape. Place some shorter
ones just off centre leaning towards the front.

Honesty should be placed asymmetrically,
allowing the light to shine through the seed
heads. Keep a few short pieces for later.

Add the strong pink and sparkling white
Helipterum, again making sure that they are not
too symmetrical, with some flowers sideways
and others downwards.

Once most of the plants are in place, check
that the general shape is pleasing and balanced
but not too formal from every angle, including
the view through the window.

As a finishing touch, drape short pieces of
Gypsophila, honesty and *Helipterum* over the
edge of the container to soften the effect and
diagonally counterbalance any slight 'over-
weight' on the left or right side of the
arrangement.

PRACTICAL HINT
Dried flowers left in bright light will fade more
quickly than those away from a window, but this
arrangement should last for up to a year unless it
is in hot sunshine.

Freshness and light are the twin themes of this deceptively artless vase of old

favourites – country flowers with wheat.

INGREDIENTS
Ordinary green 'sack' moss (Mnium) – 1–2 large packets
Silvery reindeer moss (Cladonia rangiferina) – 1–2 large packets
Lavender (Lavendula spica) – 6–7 bunches
Lavender pot pourri – 1 large packet

EQUIPMENT
Circular basket 10 in (25 cm) diameter, 4 in (10 cm) deep; tissue paper; 1 ft (30 cm)-wide fine-gauge chicken wire; reel wire; stub/florists' wire – 1 packet green medium gauge; raffia; wire-cutters; scissors.

METHOD
Make a moss and chicken wire ring base (see p. 17) about 2 in (5 cm) in diameter to go round the top of the basket and attach it to the outer rim by threading a piece of stub/florists' wire through the inside edge of the base, through the wickerwork and then twisting the two wire ends together tightly. Do this at least 6 times, so that the base will not come adrift later.

Cover the ring base with clumps of reindeer moss, leaving small gaps round the bases of the handle and round the ring where 4 of the crossed bunches of lavender will go. Attach the moss with U-shaped pieces of stub/florists' wire.

Make 14 small bunches of lavender, each trimmed to a maximum of 5 in (12.5 cm) long.

(Save the stalks, if they are long enough, for another arrangement.) Using a strand of raffia, tie each bunch neatly with a bow round the middle.

The bunches are attached to the base by U-shaped pieces of stub/florists' wire looped through the raffia at the back of each bunch. The bottom bunch is affixed first with the second wired through the bottom one into the base.

The crossed bunches are placed as follows: (1) round the handle base, both bunches have their heads pointing into the centre of the basket; (2) both bunches have their heads pointing outwards; (3) 1 head points inwards, the other outwards; (4) round the other handle base, both heads point inwards; (5) 1 head points inwards and 1 outwards; and (6) both heads point outwards.

The last 2 bunches are tied to the basket handle with stub/florists' wire and/or raffia, their heads pointing upwards.

Smooth out several layers of tissue paper inside the basket and cover it thickly with lavender pot pourri.

PRACTICAL HINT
The more tissue paper there is in the basket, the fuller it will seem whilst also saving the cost of large amounts of pot pourri. An alternative would be to line the basket with material before beginning the arrangement.

WOODHAMS

The delights of an old-fashioned cottage garden are evoked by the incomparable fragrance of this pot pourri basket.

INGREDIENTS

Ordinary green 'sack' moss (Mnium) – 2–3 large bags
Red hybrid tea roses – 3 bunches
Lavender (Lavendula spica) – 3 bunches
Love-in-a-mist (Nigella damascena) – 4 bunches
Dudinea (Dudinea sp) – 4 bunches
Deep pink everlasting/strawflowers (Helichrysum bracteatum) – 4 bunches
Green hydrangea (Hydrangea macrophylla) – 3 heads
Marjoram (Origanum vulgare) – 3 bunches
Oregano (Origanum sp) – 2–3 bunches
Maroon peony (Paeonia lactiflora) – 1 head

EQUIPMENT

Piece of plain cloth (to line basket); coarse needle and thread; circular basket – approx. 12–15 in (30–37.5 cm) diameter; bag of pot pourri; roll of fine-gauge chicken wire; green reel wire; stub/florists' wire – 1 packet medium gauge, 1 packet fine gauge; reel of rose wire; pliers; wire-cutters; scissors.

METHOD

First you have to make a long 'sausage' of chicken wire filled with moss and tie it to the top of the basket.

Tie a short, bright piece of string or raffia to the rim of the basket to act as a marker. Measure the length of chicken wire needed by placing this marker on top of the end of the wire and rolling the rim of the basket straight along until the marker on the basket touches the chicken wire once more. Mark this point and cut off this length of wire.

Bend the chicken wire into a long sausage shape with a diameter of about $2\frac{1}{2}$–3 in (6.25–7.5 cm), trim away the excess, and with stub/florists' wire or reel wire close the 'sausage'. Firmly fill it with moss.

Line the basket with a plain piece of material stitched beneath the inside rim with needle and thread.

Bind the moss-filled 'sausage' to the rim of the basket: take the reel wire through the rim of the basket, over the 'sausage', back through the rim and so on. The 'sausage' must be stable.

Set aside 5 or so roses for the pot pourri. With the remainder, wire the individual rose heads into 10 clusters with stub/florists' wire (see p. 19) leaving 5 in (12.5 cm) wire 'stems'.

Divide the rest of the flowers into the following number of small bunches or clusters: lavender 9; *Nigella* 10; *Dudinea* 16; *Helichrysum* 9 (wire individual heads first if you wish, see p. 18); hydrangea 6; purple marjoram 9; and oregano 11. Wire the clusters using stub/florists' wire (see p. 19), trim the stalks and leave a 5 in (12.5 cm) wire 'stem' on each.

Beginning with the lavender, fix the bunches to the moss ring by pushing the wire 'stems' right through the 'sausage' to the other side and bending the ends of the wires back over the chicken wire into the moss. The more fragile the flowers, the more delicately you have to do this.

Remembering to cover all sides of the moss ring, including the inner side (to hide the edge of the lining material), insert the clusters of marjoram, oregano, *Helichrysum*, roses and hydrangea, followed by *Nigella*.

Fill the remaining gaps with *Dudinea*, gently easing it in with your fingertips, and then pop the solitary maroon peony somewhere on the inner rim.

Finally fill the centre of the basket with pot pourri and scatter on top the 5 spare roses.

PRACTICAL HINT

By making a shallow material lining which does not touch the bottom of the basket, less pot pourri will be needed to make it look full.

PARTERRE

All the colour and fragrance of summer days in a pot pourri basket which looks gorgeous throughout the year in a sitting or dining room.

INGREDIENTS

Ordinary green 'sack' moss (Mnium) – 3 large packets
Pale reindeer moss (Cladonia rangiferina) – 2 large packets
Protea repens – 12 heads
Leucodendron pubescens – 14 heads
Leucodendron plumosum – 15 heads
Dark brown seed pods – 13 heads
Coral fern – 5 handfuls
Brown Timothy grass (Phleum pratense) or Lamarcia or Polypogon – 5 bunches
Brown and white fern (Dryopteris sp) – 5 pieces
Lotus flower (fruit) (Nelumbo lucifera) – 25 heads, large
Pot pourri – 2 medium packets
Hazel nuts and sweet chestnuts – 1 packet of each

EQUIPMENT

Circular basket approx. 12 in (30 cm) diameter; 12 in (30 cm)-wide fine-gauge chicken wire; reel wire; stub/florists' wire – 2 packets medium gauge; wire-cutters; scissors; brown tissue paper.

METHOD

Make a moss and chicken wire base (see p. 17) to go round the basket, but make it into a flattened sausage shape about 1½ in (4 cm) thick (front to back) and about 3 in (7.5 cm) deep so that it covers the sides of the basket. Attach the base with reel wire both to the outside rim of the basket and lower down the side by threading the wire backwards and forwards through the wickerwork and the base.

Cover the base with clumps of reindeer moss affixed by U-shaped pieces of stub/florists' wire. Remember to cover the lower curve of the base.

Trim the stalks of the *Protea*, *Leucodendron* and seed pods, and wind a piece of stub/florists' wire round each stalk to leave a wire 'stem' of about 3 in (7.5 cm) (see pp. 19–20). Place these heads in groups of 3 round the basket, inserting the wire 'stems' at an angle into the moss base.

Make 5 wired bunches (see p. 19) of coral fern with wire 'stems' approximately 4–5 in (10–12.5 cm) long. Place them at various angles so that the coral fern points upwards, sideways or downwards. If the wire 'stems' penetrate the inside of the basket, simply bend the wire back round through the wickerwork into the moss.

The brown grass is wired into 5 graded bunches (see p. 19), the stalks trimmed to about 2 in (5 cm) long with a wire 'stem' of 4 in (10 cm). Insert them with the heads of the bunches upwards.

The ends of the stalks of the contorted ferns are each bound with a piece of stub/florists' wire to leave a wire 'stem' of 4 in (10 cm) and again placed at various angles amongst the other ingredients.

The dark lotus heads have their stalks trimmed to about 2–3 in (5–7.5 cm) and are wired into bunches (see p. 19) of threes or fives. These are placed wherever there is a remaining gap, some pointing upwards, some down.

Finally, spread the tissue paper so that it lines and almost completely fills the interior of the basket. Spread the pot pourri over the tissue paper to conceal it and then scatter the shiny brown nuts over the surface.

PRACTICAL HINT

If any of the ingredients are not readily available in your area, you can either order them from one of the suppliers listed at the back of this book or be imaginative about possible substitutes. Cinnamon sticks or tree twigs could replace the coral fern, cones and spray-painted artichoke heads might do instead of *Protea* and *Leucodendron*, etc.

WOODHAMS

Strangely shaped exotic plants in almost every tone of brown highlight the homeliness of the nuts and pot pourri in this masterly creation.

INGREDIENTS

Pinky green sorghum/millet (Gramina sp) – 1–2
bunches
Mauve wheat (Triticum) – 1 bunch
Opium poppy seedheads (Papaver somniferum) –
1 bunch
Burgundy safflower (Carthamus sp) – 1 bunch
Pink yarrow (Achillea ptarmica) – 1 bunch
Artificial silk roses – 5
Spiky green love-in-a-mist (Nigella orientalis) – 1
bunch
Grass (Gramina sp) – ¹/₂ bunch

EQUIPMENT

Circular basket 9 in (22.5 cm) diameter, about 4 in (10 cm) deep; dry foam – 2 blocks; adhesive tape; stub/florists' wire – 1 packet medium gauge; wire-cutters; scissors; knife.

METHOD

Trim the dry foam into a mound which will fit into the basket and tape it in position in the centre (see p. 15).

Since the strong spikes of sorghum/millet define the basic shape, remove any leaves on the lower half of the stalks and insert them into the foam.

Using 3 or 5 heads per cluster, make up about 13 wired, graded bunches of wheat (see pp. 19–20) and insert them at random intervals all over the basket. Bend the wire 'stems' of some to allow them to lean out over the rim.

The poppy seedheads are grouped in threes and fours into about 5 wired bunches, as above, and placed around the edge.

If the safflower stalks seem strong enough, insert them individually and in groups in the foam – single ones around the rim with at least 1 near the centre; the rest in threes and fives round the middle.

If the safflower stalks are weak, wire some individual heads and others in clusters, all as you would a loosely wired bunch (see pp. 19–20), and insert them in the foam as above.

Divide the pink yarrow into 5 small bunches and wire them. Scatter these small bunches amongst the arrangement.

The artificial roses are inserted next, followed by a number of small wired bunches of *Nigella orientalis*.

Individual spears of grass punctuate the arrangement and provide a light finishing touch.

PRACTICAL HINT

This is a relatively robust arrangement. Freeze-dried roses or good quality dried peonies are only two of many possible alternatives to silk roses, but, of course, they are more fragile.

AROMAROUND

Town meets country on a dresser – the strong shapes of dried plants, some dyed rich

hues, provide a satisfying foil for sensuous red silk roses.

INGREDIENTS
Lavender (Lavendula spica) – 7–9 bunches

EQUIPMENT
3 terracotta clay flowerpots – approx. 7 in (17.5 cm), 6 in (15 cm) and 5 in (12.5 cm) diameter; dry foam – 2–3 blocks; stub/florists' wire – 2 packets fine gauge; cane – approx. 3 ft (90 cm) long; wire-cutters; scissors; knife.

METHOD
Shape the dry foam so that it fills three-quarters of each pot.

Stand the pots one inside the other with the smallest on top and push a sturdy cane through the centre of the foam in the top pot until the cane goes right down through the drainage holes to the bottom of the lowest pot. This will ensure stability.

From the lavender make short, even-headed, wired bunches (see p. 19) using about 10 heads and leaving wire 'stems' about 3 in (7.5 cm) long.

Starting with the top pot, insert the bunches as close to each other as possible, keeping the heads reasonably even. On the rim you have to squeeze the bunches in delicately. To encourage the lavender to splay outwards, insert the wire 'stems' at a slight angle and wire the stalks nearer the trimmed end.

Continue inserting wired bunches of lavender in both of the other pots. When it all seems complete, make one last eagle-eyed check that no wiring is apparent and that there are no gaps.

PRACTICAL HINT
Instead of using only lavender, you could choose 3 varieties of scented plants in different colours, e.g. lavender, thyme and marjoram, or simply 3 layers of less expensive red broom bloom or yellow *Helipterum sandfordii*, for instance.

PARTERRE

JEANETTE COLLINS

A tower shape, which makes the most of limited space, elicits admiring comments and is suitable for a wide variety of plants.

INGREDIENTS
Deep pink large roses – 1 bunch
Pearl everlasting (Anaphalis) – 2 bunches
*Dark red everlasting/strawflowers (Helichrysum
    bracteatum) – 2 bunches*
Lavender (Lavendula spica) – 3 bunches
Marjoram (Origanum vulgare) – 2 bunches
*Blue hydrangea (Hydrangea macrophylla) – 2
    medium heads*
Senecio (Senecio greyi) – 1/2 bunch
Orange-pink Dudinea (Dudinea sp) – 2 sprays
Maroon peonies (Paeonia lactiflora) – 6 heads
Rose or other stalks – approx. 7 bunches

EQUIPMENT
Dry-foam sphere (from florist) – approx. 5 in
(12.5 cm) diameter; dry-foam cone (from florist)
– at least 10 in (25 cm) high; paper ribbon – 1 yd
(90 cm); cold glue or glue-gun; stub/florists'
wire – 2 packets medium gauge; green reel wire;
reel florists' adhesive tape; pliers; wire-cutters;
scissors; knife.

METHOD
Cut the top off the dry-foam cone to create a 3 in
(7.5 cm) wide platform and then glue the foam
ball firmly on top.

Divide the flowers into approximately the
following number of wired clusters using stub/
florists' wire (see p. 19): roses 6 (it is not impera-
tive to wire individual heads); *Anaphalis* 8; *Helichrysum* 3 (wire individual heads first, if
preferred); lavender 9; marjoram 6; hydrangea 7;
Senecio 3; and *Dudinea* 6. Trim the wire 'stems'
to about 3 in (7.5 cm).

The key thing to avoid when deciding where
to place each flower cluster is creating rows of,
say roses or peonies, at the same height all the
way round, so put each cluster or head higher or
lower than the previous one of the same flower.

Since the peonies and *Helichrysum* comprise
the darkest patches of colour, insert them into
the dry-foam sphere first. Then add the clusters
of lavender and marjoram. Do not be afraid to
put them beside each other occasionally.

Scatter the clusters of white *Anaphalis* round
the stook head, and do the same with the roses,
Senecio, *Dudinea* and lastly the particularly fragile hydrangea until the sphere is covered.

If you are using rose stalks, wrap one end of a
length of stub/florists' wire round the end of
each individual stalk, trim the long wire 'stem' to
about 2 in (5 cm), and bend the wire so that it
will be pointing downwards behind the stalk
when you insert it into the foam cone just beneath the sphere.

If you are using other kinds of stalks, wire
them into small, tight bunches (see p. 19) and
proceed as above.

Make sure that the stalks conceal the foam
cone, particularly round the base.

Run a band of strong adhesive tape round the
tops of the stalks, over the wiring. This helps to
fix the stalks securely.

Tie a length of green reel wire firmly round
the stalks three-quarters of the way down. Do
not let the wire cut into the stalks; it should be
left there for a couple of weeks or so to ensure
the stalks do not start warping.

Finally tie a length of good quality paper ribbon round the 'waist' of the stook, where the
two ends cross, staple them into the foam with a
piece of U-shaped stub/florists' wire. Trim the
two ends. Make a generous bow – no need for a
knot first – and pin it with wire at the back
through the cross-over into the stook. Check
that the stalk heads and wires are concealed.

PRACTICAL HINT
For added stability run a cane or a poker wire
from the top of the bare sphere through to the
base of the cone.

Singly or in pairs, luscious stooks of flowers in subtle colours that complement

those of your home will enhance a side table or mantelpiece in any room.

INGREDIENTS
Eucalyptus baby (Eucalyptus sp) – 10 bunches
Maroon peonies (Paeonia lactiflora) – 10 blooms
Peach hybrid tea roses – 5 bunches
Marjoram (Origanum vulgare) – 6 bunches
Pink-tinged green hydrangea (Hydrangea
  macrophylla) – 9 heads

EQUIPMENT
Oval basket – approx. 18 in (45 cm) × 12 in (30 cm); dry foam – 2–3 blocks; stub/florists' wire – 2–3 packets medium gauge; adhesive tape; wire-cutters; pliers; scissors; knife.

METHOD
Trim the foam blocks as necessary to fill the basket and fix in position with adhesive tape (see p. 15).

The eucalyptus is put in position first. Wrap stub/florists' wire round the ends of the eucalyptus and stick the 4 in (10 cm) wire 'stems' into the foam all round the edge of the basket. Group it more thickly in some places than others.

Then start inserting the flowers around the top centre, beginning with the peonies.

If you have the patience, wire up the individual rose heads (see p.18); if not, simply wire them into 10 small bunches (see p. 19). Place them at irregular intervals round the basket.

The marjoram should be divided into lots of loose clusters and wired with stub/florists' wire (see pp. 19–20), with 4 in (10 cm) wire 'stems'.

Lastly, because they are so fragile, delicately ease the hydrangea heads into place.

PRACTICAL HINT
This arrangement would also look marvellous in the middle of a large dining table.

PARTERRE

This lush basket of flowers pleases both

with its scent of marjoram and its

subtle combination of colours and shapes.

INGREDIENTS (for 1 stook)
*Red hybrid tea roses – 3 bunches (60) medium-
    sized blooms*
Marjoram (Origanum vulgare) – 2 bunches
Rose stalks – approx. 3 bunches

EQUIPMENT
Dry-foam sphere (from florist) approx. 5 in
(12.5 cm) diameter; dry-foam cone (from florist)
approx. 10 in (25 cm) high; cold glue; stub/
florists' wire – 9–10 packets medium gauge; reel
of adhesive tape; green reel wire; poker wire or
bamboo cane – about 18 in (30 cm) long; velvet
or silk ribbon – 1 yd (90 cm); pliers; wire-
cutters; scissors; knife.

METHOD
Using stub/florists' wire, all the individual rose
heads should be wired (see p. 18), leaving a
'stem' of about 4 in (10 cm). Keep the rose stalks
for later, and save the leaves for another
arrangement.

Divide the purple marjoram into approximately 11 short, trimmed bunches, wire them
with stub/florists' wire (see p. 19) and leave a
wire 'stem' of about 4 in (10 cm).

Cut the tip off the dry-foam cone to make a
slightly curved platform about 3 in (7.5 cm)
across, on to which the dry-foam sphere is glued
firmly. (For extra stability, if you wish, run a
length of poker wire or cane from the top of the
sphere through to the base of cone and trim both
ends of the wire or cane neatly.)

Beginning at the top and working downwards,
insert the rose heads all over the sphere, leaving
gaps between them.

Amongst the roses insert the clusters of marjoram until no dry foam is visible.

Now for the rose stalks: wrap one end of a
piece of stub/florists' wire round the end of a
rose stalk, trim the long wire 'stem' to about 2 in
(5 cm) and bend the wire down towards the stalk
so that the wire 'stem' is inserted into the foam
conc at a downward angle just below the sphere.

Do the same with the rest of the rose stalks
until the cone is covered all round and no foam is
visible. Trim the stalks round the base.

Run a band of strong adhesive tape round the
top of the stalks to cover the wiring and secure
the stalks.

To prevent the stalks warping, tie a length of
green reel wire round them three-quarters of the
way down. This can be removed when the stalks
seem stable.

Run a length of ribbon round the 'waist' of the
stook to cover the taped stalk heads, staple the
cross-over point with a U-shaped piece of stub/
florists' wire and trim the ends. Take the remaining length of ribbon and – without tying a knot
first – make a generous double bow. Hook a
longer U-shaped piece of stub/florists' wire
through the back of the bow and pin the wire
through the ribbon cross-over on the stook.

PRACTICAL HINT
Roses will open fully if you hold them in the
steam above a pan of boiling water. If you do
this with the above stook, for instance, far fewer
roses will be needed, thus saving on the cost. It is
also a handy way of covering any dry foam still
visible in this or other arrangements. The roses
become more susceptible to damage, however.

PARTERRE

Wherever you put them, the clear-cut forms of a pair of dashing red rose stooks

are a delight to the eye.

INGREDIENTS
Red Celosia cockscomb (Celosia argentea
  cristata) – 5 pieces
Pink Protea bud/Cape honey flower (Protea
  compacta) – 2 heads
Eucalyptus baby (Eucalyptus sp) – 1 bunch (10
  pieces)
Spiky green love-in-a-mist (Nigella orientalis) –
  ¹/₂ bunch
Dark blue delphinium (Delphinium sp) – ¹/₂
  bunch
White delphinium (Delphinium sp) – ¹/₂ bunch
Blue hydrangea (Hydrangea macrophylla) – 1
  head
Red Russian/rat's tail statice (Limonium
  suworowii) – 1–2 bunches
Red floribunda roses – 1 bunch
Protea repens flat – 7 heads
Orange-tipped safflower/dyer's saffron
  (Carthamus tinctorius) – 1 bunch
Opium poppy seedheads (Papaver somniferum)
  – 2
Bronze small-leaved eucalyptus (Eucalyptus sp)
  – ¹/₂ bunch (2 sprays)
Wheat (Triticum) – ¹/₂ bunch
Golden yarrow (Achillea filipendulina) – 7 small
  heads

EQUIPMENT
Bark-covered circular container – 9 in (22.5 cm)
diameter; dry foam – 2 blocks; adhesive tape;
stub/florists' wire – 1 packet medium gauge, 1
packet fine gauge; wire-cutters; scissors; knife.

METHOD
Make a well-curved mound from the dry foam
big enough to fill the container and secure it with
adhesive tape (see p. 15).

Remember that the finished arrangement is
basically a shallow cone and that the overall
height, including the container will be about
10 in (25 cm).

Begin by inserting 1 red *Celosia*, a spiky pink
Protea bud and a piece of blue eucalyptus in the
centre.

Using fine-gauge stub/florists' wire, make
the spiky green *Nigella* into 5 loose clusters ▷

MCQUEEN'S

Liven up a dull spot

with an inventive and surprising

selection of plant material

shown off in the round.

◁ (see pp. 19–20), the dark blue delphinium into 4 (inserted into the arrangement in pairs), the white delphinium into 3, the head of blue hydrangea into 3, and the red spikes of *Limonium* into 9.

If the stems of the roses look weak then wire the heads using medium-gauge stub/florists'

wire (see p. 18).

The ingredients are then placed at random round the container, working from the centre outwards and downwards, angling the flowers more acutely as you approach the rim. Ensure that some heads, particularly eucalyptus and *Limonium*, break the outline.

INGREDIENTS
Green flat moss (Mnium sp) – 1 large piece
Maroon peonies (Paeonia lactiflora) – 20

EQUIPMENT
Glass tank 9 in (22.5 cm) diameter; dry foam – 2 blocks; stub/florists' wire – 1 packet medium gauge; adhesive tape; florists' spikes – 2; adhesive clay; wire-cutters; scissors; knife.

METHOD
Shape the dry foam into a square block, using adhesive tape to attach the two pieces together. There should be a gap of at least $^1/_2$ in (15 mm) between the corners of the foam and the glass container; trim the corners off the block, if necessary, to achieve it.

Using adhesive clay, secure the florists' spikes to the base of the glass tank and impale the dry foam firmly upon them.

Cover the top of the foam with moss stapled in place with short U-shaped pieces of stub/florists' wire.

Fill the tank up to the rim with moss, easing it into place with one or more lengths of stub/florists' wire used like chopsticks to guide it. Check that no foam is visible.

If the peonies are not fully open, before trimming the stalks, hold the flowers in the steam above a boiling kettle or pan until the petals unfurl.

Trim the stalks of the peonies to leave about 1 in (2·5 cm) below each flower, wind a length of stub/florists' wire round each stalk to leave a wire 'stem' around 5 in (12.5 cm) long (see pp. 19–20).

Place 1 peony dead centre, and then set 6 peonies around it. The final 13 go round the edge.

Check again that the dry foam is still hidden by the moss and that the flowers are evenly spaced.

PRACTICAL HINT
Instead of filling the tank with moss, simply use some to cover the top of the dry foam and then fill the sides with a prettily coloured pot pourri.

Pale pink peonies, stemless thistle flowers (*Carlina acaulis* 'Caulescens'), roses or small hydrangea heads also look well displayed in this way.

JULIET WILLIS

For supreme elegance and simplicity it is hard to beat jewel-like peonies in sparkling glass on a dark sideboard or table.

INGREDIENTS

*Ordinary green 'sack' moss (Mnium) – 3 or
  more large packets*
Love-in-a-mist (Nigella damascena) – 3 bunches
Maroon hybrid tea roses – 1 bunch
Marjoram (Origanum vulgare) – 2 bunches
*Wine red broom bloom (Gypsophila rugosa) – 3
  bunches*
*Pink-tinged blue hydrangea (Hydrangea
  macrophylla) – 3 medium heads*
Orange-pink Dudinea (Dudinea sp) – 1 spray
*Pink everlasting/strawflowers (Helichrysum sp)
  – 2 bunches*

EQUIPMENT

1 metal wreath frame (from florist); church
candle; glass candle-jar; green string; stub/
florists' wire – 1–2 packets medium gauge; reel
of fine rose wire; wire-cutters; scissors.

METHOD

Remember to check that the candle-jar will fit in
the centre of the wreath frame.

Cover the wreath frame with moss, binding it
on with string (see p. 17). Do not forget to cover
the inside, where it will be visible through the
glass jar.

Divide the flowers into the following approxi-
mate number of clusters and wire them (see p.
19), leaving about 4 in (10 cm) wire as a stem:
Nigella 8; roses 5 (wire the individual heads if
you wish, as on p. 18); marjoram 8; broom
bloom 9; hydrangea 7; and *Dudinea* 4. Wire the
heads of pink *Helichrysum* (see p. 18), if you
wish, and then wire them into 6 clusters.

Begin by inserting all the clusters of, for instance, the strong red broom bloom in a hapha-
zard zigzag, with alternately one at the top and
one at the bottom. Press the wire 'stem' of each
cluster through the wreath and then bend the
protruding end neatly back into the moss.

Avoid putting all the clusters of one type of
flower at the same height all the way round.
Turn the wreath as you gently insert the hydrangeas and other wire clusters closely, up and
down.

Delicately insert the 4 clusters of *Dudinea*
wherever you think most effective. Any left-over
Helichrysum, etc., can also be used to fill any
small gaps.

Finally, place the candle-jar and candle in the
centre of the wreath.

PRACTICAL HINT

Avoid using a dry-foam ring for the base as it
tends to be far too fragile and breaks up easily.

PARTERRE

Whether you are having a relaxed meal or a more formal dinner party, the gemlike

colours of this centrepiece will glow by day as well as by night.

INGREDIENTS
White baby's breath (Gypsophila) – 3 bunches
White sea lavender (Limonium sp) – 3 bunches
Dark blue everlasting/strawflowers
  (Helichrysum bracteatum) – 3 bunches
Silver everlasting/strawflowers (Helichrysum
  vestium) – 1 bunch
Cream sunray/Rhodanthe (Helipterum
  manglesii) – 1 bunch
Blue sea holly (Eryngium sp) – 1 bunch
Natural wheat (Triticum) – 1 bunch
Green love-lies-bleeding (Amaranthus caudatus
  'Viridis') – 1 bunch
Natural canary grass seedheads (Phalaris sp) – 1
  bunch
White Senecio (Senecio greyi) – 1 bunch
Yellow tassel flower (Cacalia sp) – 1 bunch

EQUIPMENT
Circular basket or container – approx. 7 in (17.5 cm) diameter; dry-foam cone (from florist) – approx. 10 in (25 cm) high – or 1 dry-foam block; florists' spike – 1 or more; adhesive clay; adhesive tape; stub/florists' wire – 1 packet medium gauge; reel of rose wire (in a cup); wire-cutters; scissors; knife.

METHOD
If you are using a block of dry foam, round off the corners at one end with a knife and bear in mind, when you place the flowers, that the finished arrangement is a gentle cone shape.

Using adhesive tape and a florists' spike affixed to the bottom of the container with adhesive clay, firmly secure the foam cone or block standing on end.

Trim the stalks as necessary before inserting clusters of *Gypsophila* and sea lavender all over the foam, with more of the latter round the bottom, draping over the basket rim, than on top. Do not push the stalks in too far; as you can see, the ingredients protrude at least 3 in (7.5 cm) from the base at the bottom and rather less at the top to create the cone shape.

Divide the dark blue *Helichrysum* into 11 tight wired bunches (see p. 19) and spread them round the foam.

Next wire the heads of silver *Helichrysum* and cream sunray (see p. 18), unless you think they are sturdy enough not to need this, and scatter them all over the arrangement.

Pieces of blue sea holly are widely dispersed, as are the more pointed shapes of individual heads of wheat, *Amaranthus* and *Phalaris*.

Clusters of white *Senecio* fill any remaining gaps and then the arrangement is delicately punctuated with small pieces of yellow tassel flower.

Lastly, check that there are no remaining gaps through which the dry foam can be seen and, if the outline seems too solid or regular, insert a few pieces of *Gypsophila* to soften the effect.

PRACTICAL HINT
Most of the ingredients in this arrangement are quite inexpensive and colours other than blue and yellow would be equally effective, providing they do not clash with the decor of the room.

Even without silver dishes supporting it, this light and graceful centrepiece has an

air of glamour and luxury which belies its cost.

INGREDIENTS

Dark pink peonies (Paeonia lactiflora) – 7
flowers
Purple marjoram (Origanum vulgare) – 1
bunch
Green love-lies-bleeding (Amaranthus caudatus
'Viridis') – 1–2 bunches
Dark pink hybrid tea roses – 1 bunch
Cream hybrid tea roses – 3 flowers
Eucalyptus baby (Eucalyptus sp) – 1/2 bunch
Pink delphinium (Delphinium sp) – 1 head
Red copper beech leaves (Fagus sylvatica
'Cuprea') – 1 large branch or 11 small pieces

EQUIPMENT

Reel of rose wire (in a cup); stub/florists' wire –
1 packet medium gauge; (optional) dry foam – 1/2
block; (optional) jam jar; adhesive tape; crimson
ribbon; scissors.

METHOD

The posy is built into a dome from the centre
outwards, in rough circles of ingredients. Most
arrangers hold the growing posy in their hand,
but you may find it feasible to sculpt a piece of
dry foam into a sharp dome to put in a jam jar
and then hold the ingredients with the stalks
resting on the foam. The dome of foam will push
up the heads in the centre and so help to create
the dome shape of the posy.

In the centre you start with a peony sur-
rounded by 5 pieces of marjoram and 5
Amaranthus. Every time you add 3 or 4 flowers,
bind the posy with rose wire – do not cut the
wire as this wastes time.

Remember you are creating a dome shape.
Next come 6 pink and 2 cream roses, followed
by more marjoram and *Amaranthus*. Keep on
binding in the additions with the rose wire.

The blue eucalyptus baby, pieces of pink delphinium and the rest of the peonies are added at
random so that the posy does not look too
contrived.

The red copper beech leaves are used as an
encircling frame. If the twigs do not seem the
right shape, wire the leaves in pairs by pushing a
piece of stub/florists' wire through the bases and
twisting the short wire end round the long wire
to tie them together.

Tie the final layer of the bunch firmly, but not
so tightly as to break the stalks.

Cover the encircling wire with adhesive tape,
again tying it fairly firmly to help keep the ingredients in place.

Finally tie a length of ribbon over the tape,
making a double bow, and trim the plant stalks
evenly. Also trim off any wire ends still visible.

PRACTICAL HINT

The marjoram and eucalyptus already have a
subtle, lovely scent, but a few drops of essential
oil would add impact.

MCQUEEN'S

This effervescent posy was inspired by the Victorians, who were not as timid in

their choice of colours as many still believe.

INGREDIENTS
Blue hydrangea (Hydrangea macrophylla) – 1
    large head
Green reindeer moss (Cladonia rangiferina)
    – 1 medium packet
Opium poppy seedheads (Papaver somniferum)
    – 3
Cream floribunda roses – 4 heads
Green sea lavender (Limonium sp) – 1/2 bunch
Fir cones – 4 small to medium
Artificial fruit – 1 pear, 1 cluster blackberries,
    2 clusters black grapes
Miniature baskets – 2
Miniature terracotta clay flowerpots – 3
Cloves – 1–2 packets
Cinnamon sticks – 4
Magnolia leaves – approx. 11

EQUIPMENT
Stub/florists' wire – 1 packet long, medium gauge; reel of brown gutta-percha tape; dry foam – 1/2 block; cold glue; raffia – 2 strands; reel of Stemtex or similar brown adhesive binding tape; red velvet ribbon – 1/4 in (0.7 cm) wide, 3 yds (2.7 m); florists' scissors; ribbon scissors; wire-cutters; pliers; knife.

METHOD
Divide the hydrangea head in half and wire each with stub/florists' wire (see p. 19), leaving a wire stem of approximately 8 in (20 cm).

In similar fashion wire up: 7 clumps of moss; 1 cluster of 3 poppy heads; each rose head separately (see p. 18); 3 clusters of sea lavender; each fir cone (see p. 19); and each piece of fruit. Bind the top half of each wire 'stem' in gutta-percha (see p. 19).

Loop one end of a piece of stub/florists' wire through the bottom of each miniature basket and gutta-percha the 'stems' as above.

Twist a piece of wire round a tiny twig or matchstick and slip it through the hole at the bottom of each flowerpot so that the twig forms an anchor to secure the wire. Shape pieces of dry foam to fill 2 of the pots and glue firmly in place. Disguise the foam by glueing on a mass of cloves. Bind all 3 wire 'stems' in gutta-percha.

Chop the 4 cinnamon sticks in half and make into 2 bunches tied with raffia; attach an 8 in (20 cm) length of stub/florists' wire to each and bind with gutta-percha as above.

About $\frac{3}{4}$ in (1.9 cm) from the top of a magnolia leaf, stitch a length of stub/florists' wire through from the back, over the top of the central vein and back down again through the leaf. Slide the wire along until the 'stitch' is in the centre of the wire and carefully bend the two ends of wire in a fairly tight U down towards the leaf stem, so that the wire lies flat against the back of the leaf. With the leaf surface facing you, gently bend the leaf and its wire backwards in the middle, thus curving the leaf. Do the same with each of the remaining magnolia leaves.

Gather the various ingredients into a posy with the magnolia leaves forming an overlapping ring round the edge. Wire the whole bunch together firmly.

Trim or bend back any wire 'stems' which are much longer than the others, but leave a handle of approx 3 in (7.5 cm). Bind the handle in bark-coloured adhesive tape.

Cut the velvet ribbon into 3 equal lengths and tie them into large double bows. Make 3 long 'hairpins' of stub/florists' wire, thread one through each bow, twist the wire round tightly several times beneath each bow and then insert each into the posy.

PRACTICAL HINT
If you stand the wired ingredients in a narrow-necked jar or container while arranging them, it will be much easier.

PARTERRE

An eclectic modern posy makes an unusual conversation piece and is an original way

of using up odds and ends.

INGREDIENTS
Branch – approx. 12 in (30 cm) long
Sphagnum moss – 1 large packet
Scots pine cones (Pinus sylvestris) – approx. 80
medium-sized
Ordinary green 'sack' moss (Mnium) – 1 small
packet

EQUIPMENT
Terracotta clay pot – approx. 6 in (15 cm) diameter; plaster of Paris or quick-drying cement – 1 packet; water; mixing bowl or bucket and stirring implement; slices of foam to line pot if using plaster of Paris; dry-foam cone (from a florist) – approx. 9 in (22.5 cm) high; brown stub/florists' wire – 4 packets fine gauge; cold glue; pliers; wire-cutters; knife.

METHOD
Either three-quarters fill the pot with a mix of quick-drying cement, or line the pot with slices of foam and then three-quarters fill it with a thick, creamy mix of plaster of Paris, making sure the foam stays in place. (Plaster of Paris expands as it sets, so the foam will allow for this and prevent the pot cracking.)

Cement and plaster dry quickly, so put the mixing bowl and stirrer to soak as soon as you have finished with them, otherwise they will be ruined or crack.

Gently tap the bottom of the pot on a table to settle the cement or plaster and swiftly insert the branch in the middle to form a miniature tree trunk; wobble it around a couple of times to ensure adhesion. Supporting the tree trunk with one hand, rotate the pot with the other to check that the trunk looks vertical from all angles. Hold or prop up the trunk vertically until the cement or plaster is dry and hard.

Press the foam cone on to the top of the trunk so that the size of the trunk's diameter is indented in the foam. With a sharp knife cut out the foam inside the outline to a depth of about 2 in (5 cm). Impale the foam firmly on the trunk and cover it with patches of moss stapled by U-shaped pieces of stub/florists' wire.

Using brown stub/florists' wire, wire the cones (see p. 19). Trim the short end tidily and, if necessary, trim the long wire to about 3 in (7.5 cm).

Stick the wired fir cones into the foam, working from the top downwards. Some cones should protrude further than others to give a natural look, but they should all be close together.

To finish off the tree, glue small clumps of fresh-looking green moss around the base of the trunk.

PRACTICAL HINT
A tree made of white statice (*Limonium* sp), as shown opposite, is much simpler and quicker to make. The silver strawberry (*Leptospermum* sp) tree (right) looks good enough to eat, but is more costly and more fragile.

Fir-cone trees have the enduring appeal of a piece of sculpture, yet this type of tree

looks equally effective when made with other ingredients.

INGREDIENTS

Tree branch – approx. 10 in (25 cm) long

Yellow/orange reindeer moss (Cladonia rangiferina) – 1 large packet

Black reindeer moss (Cladonia rangiferina) – 1 medium packet

Green sphagnum moss – 1 small packet

EQUIPMENT

Terracotta clay pot 5 in (12.5 cm) diameter, 4 in (10 cm) high; 1 packet plaster of Paris or quick-drying cement; mixing bowl; stirrer; dry foam – $\frac{1}{2}$ block; dry-foam sphere (from florist) 4 in (10 cm) diameter; cold glue; stub/florists' wire – 1 packet medium gauge; wire-cutters; scissors; knife.

METHOD

The overall height of the finished pom-pom tree will be about 13 in (32.5 cm).

Either three-quarters fill the terracotta clay pot with quick-drying cement, or line the pot with slices of dry foam and then three-quarters fill it with a thick mix of plaster of Paris. (The foam prevents the plaster, which expands as it dries, from cracking the pot.)

Quickly rinse the mixing bowl and stirrer, and return to the pot.

Tap the bottom of the pot on the table a couple of times to ensure the mixture has settled.

Insert one end of the miniature tree trunk in the centre with its end resting on the bottom of the pot. Twist it round several times so that the trunk is well coated with setting mixture and to check that it is vertical.

Hold or prop up the trunk in a vertical position until the plaster or cement is dry and hard.

Press the dry-foam sphere gently, with a twisting motion, on to the top of the trunk until the trunk is approximately half-way through the ball. To ensure adhesion, remove the trunk again, put some glue on it and replace it inside the ball.

Using U-shaped pieces of stub/florists' wire, staple small, compact bunches of yellow moss to the foam, leaving gaps for the black moss.

Affix the black moss using the same method in compact blobs and squiggles.

Trim the whole surface of the sphere with very sharp scissors so that the outline is smooth.

Glue small clumps of green moss round the base of the trunk.

PRACTICAL HINT

Dyed moss is available in many colours, so this idea can be adapted to suit your own colour scheme. A pair look striking on a mantelpiece. Purple marjoram (*Oreganum vulgare*), yellow *Sanfordii* or *Helichrysum italicum*, tightly packed, are alternative coverings.

...TRACEY FOR JULIET WILLIS

This witty and sophisticated pom-pom tree makes a stunning feature whether the surroundings are ancient or modern.

INGREDIENTS

Tree branch – approx. 4 ft (1.2 m) long

Sphagnum moss – 1 medium packet

Pale pink Swan River everlasting (Helipterum manglesii) – 7 bunches

Pink globe Amaranth (Gomphrena globosa) – 4 bunches

Silver everlasting/strawflowers (Helichrysum vestium) – 6 bunches

Pale salmon-pink statice (Limonium sp) – 2 bunches

Deep salmon-pink statice (Limonium sp) – 2 bunches

White sea lavender (Limonium sp) – 1 bunch

Pink ti tree/willow myrtle (Agonis juniperina) – 2 bunches

White delphinium (Delphinium sp) – 2 bunches

Cerise-tinged hybrid tea roses (Rosa 'Mercedes') – 1 bunch

EQUIPMENT

Circular container – approx. 7 in (17.5 cm) diameter; dry-foam sphere (from florist) or make your own ball using chicken wire and moss (see p. 16) – approx. 6–7 in (15–17.5 cm) diameter; plaster of Paris and ½ block of dry foam, or quick-drying cement; mixing bowl and stirring implement; stub/florists' wire – 1–2 packets long, medium gauge; staple gun or adhesive tape; pink ribbon; glue gun or cold glue; wire-cutters; scissors; knife.

METHOD

If you are using plaster of Paris, line the container with slices of dry foam to prevent it cracking as the plaster dries. Make a thick mix of plaster or cement and fill three-quarters of the container.

Quickly rinse the mixing bowl and stirrer before the mix sets on them.

Tap the bottom of the container on the work surface a couple of times to ensure that there are no air bubbles in the mixture and insert the tree branch. Twist the 'trunk' back and forth several times so that it is well coated with the mix, and check that it is vertical. Hold or prop up the trunk until the plaster or cement is set fast.

If you have bought one, press the dry-foam ball firmly on to the top of the trunk and cover it with a thin layer of moss affixed by U-shaped pieces of stub-florists' wire.

If you are making your own moss and chicken wire ball, follow the instructions on p. 16, but leave a gap in the wire through which to insert the trunk. Staple the ball to the trunk or tie it on with adhesive tape and then cover it in moss attached by U-shaped pieces of stub/florists' wire.

Divide the following ingredients into the number of small, graded, wired bunches (see p. 19) specified after each: from 5 of the 7 bunches of Helipterum – 12; globe Amaranth – 11; silver *Helichrysum* – 15; pale salmon-pink statice – 7; and deep salmon-pink statice – 7. Insert these clusters randomly round the tree.

Between these ingredients insert approximately 8-in (20-cm) long pieces of sea lavender, ti tree and delphinium. They should break the rather solid outline of the clusters.

Fill any gaps with left-over heads, and then insert the roses at random. Wire the individual rose heads if you wish (see p. 18), but you may well find you can insert the stalks directly into the foam without the heads falling off.

Lace some ribbon around the trunk and glue it in place at top and bottom. Arrange the remaining 2 bunches of *Helipterum* round the base of the trunk and glue them in place.

As an optional finishing touch, tie 4 pieces of ribbon into generous bows and attach them to the tree with U-shaped pieces of stub/florists' wire hooked through the back of each bow.

Trees like this are a long-standing favourite not only because they look so pretty but also because their shape suits most circumstances.

INGREDIENTS

Lotus flowers (fruit) (Nelumbo lucifera) – 29 heads, small

Red love-lies-bleeding (Amaranthus sp) – 2 bunches

Copper beech (Fagus sylvatica 'Cuprea') – 5 or more leafy branches

Dark pink-striped love-in-a-mist (Nigella damascena) – 2 bunches

Spiky green love-in-a-mist (Nigella orientalis) – 2 bunches

Pink delphinium (Delphinium sp) – 2 bunches

Pink miniature sunray (Helipterum sp) – 1 bunch

Grey-green oregano (Origanum sp) – 2 bunches

Pale mauve flowering thyme (Thymus sp) – 2 bunches

White South Australian daisy (Ixodia sp) – 1/2 bunch

Cream feather flower (Verticordia sp) – 1/2 bunch

Dark red hybrid tea roses – 1 bunch

Dark pink peonies (Paeonia lactiflora) – 5 heads

Pink-tinged green hydrangea (Hydrangea macrophylla) – 14 heads

Dryandra (Dryandra quercifolia) – 3 heads with leaves

Contorted willow (Salix sp) – 1 medium branch

EQUIPMENT

Dry foam – 3 blocks; coarse-gauge chicken wire; stub/florists' wire – 2 packets medium gauge, 1 packet fine gauge; paper ribbon or similar; reel wire; green gutta-percha tape; wire-cutters; scissors; knife.

METHOD

The overall length of the base is about 4 ft (1.3 m).

Slice the dry-foam blocks in half lengthways so that each piece is about 1½ in (3.5 cm) thick.

Lay them end to end and, from the touching ends, using a sharp knife, trim narrow triangles to create a continuous curve – the shape of the swag.

Cover the whole foam base in chicken wire 'stitched' together with reel wire at the back. For safety, remember to fold any spiky wire ends into the foam so that you will not cut your fingers.

Next, cover the sides and back of the base with paper ribbon or similar fixed to the base with U-shaped pieces of medium-gauge stub/florists' wire. This both hides the base and will protect the wall on which the swag is to hang.

Attach 2 reel-wire loops with which to suspend the swag to the chicken wire at the back inner curve of the base.

Divide the following ingredients into the specified number of small, graded, wired bunches (see p. 19), using medium gauge for tougher stalks and fine gauge on thinner stalks, and cover the wiring with gutta-percha (see p. 19): Lotus – 6; red *Amaranthus* – 21; copper beech – 37, using 2 or 3 leaves in each; *Nigella damascena* – 11; *Nigella orientalis* – 10; pink delphinium – 18; pink miniature sunray – 4; oregano – 8; thyme – 7; *Ixodia* – 2; feather flower – 2; and roses – 6 (wire the individual heads first, if you prefer, see p. 18).

Wire the stalks of the peonies, hydrangea and *Dryandra* as you would a loose bunch, using medium-gauge stub/florists' wire.

Working from the centre outwards, insert the bunches of lotus, red *Amaranthus* and *Nigella damascena* at an angle along the middle of the swag with their heads pointing roughly towards the end they are nearest.

The rest of the bunches are placed where you like, but those in the centre should face more towards you and be positioned at different angles to avoid a visual break.

Finally insert short pieces of contorted willow to soften the outline, some coming out towards you.

The swag is now ready to hang.

PRACTICAL HINT

If you are using grey dry foam, there is no necessity to trim the blocks before covering them with chicken wire – you can simply bend the foam and wire into a curve. This will not work with green dry foam because it is too crumbly.

If any of the ingredients are damaged or fade over the course of time, wired bunches can easily be replaced by fresh material.

JULIET WILLIS

The opulence of this enchanting swag will turn anyone's home into a castle, distracting the eye from any shortcomings elsewhere without being overwhelming.

INGREDIENTS

Cream/peach hybrid tea roses – 2 bunches
  (about 36 heads)
Rose leaves – 5 or more
Bleached wheat (Triticum) – 1 bunch
Miniature terracotta clay pots – 2
Pale blue delphinium (Delphinium sp) – 2 heads
Mauve delphinium (Delphinium sp) – 2 heads
Bamboo leaves (Arundinaria sp) – 4, rolled
Stalks – 2 any variety

EQUIPMENT

Silver birch or vine circle base (from florist); stub/florists' wire – 1 packet fine gauge, 2 long pieces medium gauge; glue gun or cold glue; rose paper ribbon; coffee paper ribbon; scissors.

METHOD

To attach the roses either trim the stalks very short and glue the heads to the base or wire the individual heads (see p. 18) and push the wire 'stems' through the base until the wire emerges on the other side, whereupon you bend the end round and back into the base.

About 9 roses are attached in a group on the upper left-hand side.

Another 6 roses are inserted on a diagonal on the upper right-hand side. Make sure that there are roses on the inner and outer sides of the base as well as on the front, so that the illusion is created that they run right round the garland.

Rose leaves, 2 each side, are either glued in place or (less securely) affixed by U-shaped pieces of stub/florists' wire pushed through the leaves into the base.

Apart from one, the remaining roses are set in a looping string winding from inside the left of the base, down towards the outside, back up a short way, down to the outside edge left of centre, up across the centre towards the inside, down for the next 2, up towards the inside again and finally running off to the lower right-hand-side outer edge.

The last rose is placed at the bottom, just right of centre.

The heads of bleached wheat are either glued individually to the base or wired into very irregular bunches (see p. 19) of varying numbers of heads. Insert the longer pieces diagonally either side of the centre of the bottom of the garland, but avoid making the arrangement symmetrical. The shorter pieces of wheat are placed lower down.

Run a length of medium-gauge stub/florists' wire through the hole in the base of each miniature flowerpot and tie them firmly to the base, one pointing up, the other down.

Fill the pots with florets of pale delphinium glued to the bottoms and sides.

The rest of the pale blue delphinium is divided into 7 pieces, wired as you would a cluster (see pp. 19–20) and placed at irregular intervals across the lower part of the circle.

The 2 mauve delphiniums are divided into 5 pieces and wired and placed in the same way.

The basic method for making the 1 large and 2 small rosettes is by folding a length of paper ribbon double, rolling it up, tying stub/florists' wire tightly round the non-folded side of the roll and pulling the folded side gently outwards into a flower shape.

Insert the 4 rolled bamboo leaves and stalks diagonally, wiring the ends of the leaves as for a bunch (see p. 19) or glueing them in place.

PRACTICAL HINT

For any home with lively children or pets, garlands are one of the most practical arrangements to make since they are the least likely to get damaged.

Reminiscent of the Napoleonic era, this chic garland nevertheless has a very up-to-date look.

INGREDIENTS

Deep blue delphinium (Delphinium sp) – 4 flowers

Golden lady's mantle (Alchemilla mollis) – 2 bunches

Orange-tipped safflower/dyer's saffron (Carthamus tinctorius) – 3 bunches

Red everlasting/strawflowers (Helichrysum bracteatum) – 2 bunches

Wheat (Triticum) – 2 bunches

Yellow miniature chrysanthemums (Chrysanthemum sp) – 3 bunches

Lotus flower (fruit) (Nelumbo lucifera) – 4, medium

Golden mushroom – 1

Protea repens flat – 2

Chinese lantern/bladder cherry (Physalis alkekengi franchetii) – 1 bunch

EQUIPMENT

Circle base made of vines (from florist); stub/florists' wire – 1 packet medium gauge; green gutta-percha tape; glue gun (preferably) or cold glue; wire-cutters; scissors.

METHOD

Apart from the lotus flowers, golden mushroom, *Protea* and orange *Physalis*, the rest of the ingredients are made into the following number of graded, wired bunches (see p. 19) with wire 'stems' about 4–5 in (10–12.5 cm) long, and the wire is then covered in gutta-percha (see p. 19): delphinium – 10 with some quite long heads; *Alchemilla mollis* – 7; safflower – 9; *Helichrysum*

– 6; wheat – 11; and miniature chrysanthemums – 13.

With the heads pointing in one direction only – clockwise or anti-clockwise – begin by inserting bunches of delphinium, *Alchemilla mollis* and safflower at varying angles all round the wreath. Push the wire 'stems' through the base until the ends emerge, then bend them round a vine strand and back into the base to hold the clusters firmly.

As you progress, make sure that the taped lower part of the clusters is hidden by the next bunch inserted.

The red *Helichrysum*, wheat clusters and chrysanthemums are inserted next, mostly round the edges.

Wrap one end of a piece of stub/florists' wire round each of the stalks of the lotus flowers, golden mushroom and *Protea* much as you would a loose bunch (see pp. 19–20). Leave wire 'stems' about 4–5 in (10–12.5 cm) long. Some are placed on the front face, others round the sides.

Lastly the orange *Physalis* are divided into 6 clusters of 3, 4 or 5 heads and these are glued in place on the front face of the garland. Fill any remaining gaps with small wired clusters of safflower leaves.

PRACTICAL HINT

Providing the garland is kept out of strong light, away from windows, it should last for several years, though naturally the colours may fade a little. If any ingredients become too pallid, fresh clusters can be substituted.

This vivacious garland, which never dates, will immediately inject fresh life and interest into overfamiliar surroundings.

JULIET WILLIS

INGREDIENTS

Silver birch (Betula pendula) branches – approx. 7, roughly 4¹/₂ ft (1.3 m) long
Oak (Quercus) twigs with leaves – 5 or more
Bronze yarrow (Achillea filipendulina) – 1 bunch
White cluster-flowered everlasting/strawflowers (Helichrysum italicum) – 1 bunch

EQUIPMENT

Brown reel wire; stub/florists' wire – 1 packet medium gauge; rigid, waterproof gold bow and golden bauble (Christmas decorations from shop); secateurs; wire-cutters; scissors.

METHOD

If you collect your own silver birch branches, cut them off using sharp secateurs so as not to damage the tree.

Whilst they are still flexible, trim off twigs and leaves, and loosely plait the branches into a circle or pear shape (see p. 18). Leave the circle to dry out for several weeks on a flat surface.

When the base is completely dry, attach fresh or dried leafy oak twigs or individual leaves by wrapping the stems with stub/florists' wire and twining the loose end neatly into the birch. Fresh leaves are for short-term use only.

Trim the yarrow stems and attach the heads to the circle in clusters with stub/florists' wire.

Then attach varying sizes of wired bunches (see p. 19) of white *Helichrysum italicum*.

Using reel wire, make a wire loop at the top of the garland to hang it from.

For a festive look, attach a gold bow to the top of the garland with reel wire and add a golden bauble tied in the same way.

PRACTICAL HINT

To preserve leafy twigs with glycerine, trim the stems cleanly, split the ends and stand them in fresh water for 3 hours. Mix 40% glycerine with 60% very hot water and stand the stems in 3–4 in (7.5–10 cm) of the mixture. The leaves must not touch the solution. Keep the container somewhere cool and dark for about 3 weeks until the plants are dry.

JEANETTE COLLINS

To welcome guests to a festive event or a special occasion, why not make an

informal country garland for the front door?

INGREDIENTS
Orange-yellow everlasting/strawflowers (Helichrysum bracteatum) – 1 bunch
Bearded wheat (Triticum) – 1 bunch

EQUIPMENT
Stub/florists' wire – 1 packet medium gauge; (optional) reel of rose wire; (optional) green gutta-percha tape; wire-cutters; scissors; natural raffia.

METHOD
If you wish to do so, wire the individual heads of *Helichrysum* using medium-gauge stub/florists' wire and rose wire, and then bind the 'stems' with gutta-percha tape (see pp. 18 and 19).

Otherwise simply choose 1 *Helichrysum* with a strong stalk to start with and then attach another (wired or unwired) *Helichrysum* to it by winding stub/florists' wire round both the new stalk and the first one.

Gradually add more flowers with their heads pointing in all directions by wiring them as above to the previous ones until you have a 'chain' incorporating all the flowers. Trim any wire ends neatly.

Divide the bearded wheat into 3. With 1 of these arrange the heads so that they form a point and tie this bunch fairly loosely with a length of stub/florists' wire. Then add the second batch of wheat as a layer round the first, still adjusting the heads to create a pointed cone. Tie the second layer as you did the first. Then add the third and final layer of wheat, adjusting the heads and tying it as before.

Cover the wire on the wheat by tying a length of raffia round the bunch, knotting it neatly or making a bow.

Trim the ends of the wheat stalks at an acute angle.

Wrap the flower 'chain' diagonally round the wheat and attach them to each other at the top and bottom with wire tied at the back of the bunch of wheat.

Make a small wire loop at the back of the bunch from which to hang it.

PRACTICAL HINT
Hanging bunches can include any ingredients and are an amusing way of experimenting with different combinations of dried plant material without rendering it unusable for other arrangements later. This is also a popular way of drying and storing material (see p. 7).

JEANETTE COLLINS

JEANETTE COLLINS

Hanging bunches can be rustic or sophisticated to suit the surroundings and are one of the easiest, most traditional ways of displaying dried plants.

INGREDIENTS *(Front and sides only)*

Tree logs – 2, each 9 in (22.5 cm) long, 2 in (5 cm) diameter

Beige hessian bag of herbs – 1

Loaves – 7, various white and black types, approx. 8 in (20 cm) long; 1 cottage loaf; 1 square loaf – all stale, but not hard.

Bread rolls – 11 or more, various types and colours, all stale but not hard

Scallop shells – 2

Wheat (Triticum) – 5 bunches

Wild oats (Avena fatua) – 4 bunches

Golden yarrow (Achillea filipendulina) – 2–3 bunches

Birds' nests with eggs – 2

Scarlet hybrid tea roses – 2 bunches

Yellow Helipterum sandfordii – 3–4 bunches

Pink sunray (Helipterum sp) – 1 bunch

Red silver strawberry (Leptospermum sp) – 2 bunches

Orange-tipped safflower/dyer's saffron (Carthamus tinctorius) – 1 bunch

Orange-yellow everlasting/strawflowers (Helichrysum bracteatum) – 1 bunch

Very dark red everlasting/strawflowers (Helichrysum bracteatum) – 7 bunches

Lavender (Lavendula spica) – 2 bunches

Purple marjoram (Origanum vulgare) – 1 bunch

EQUIPMENT

Circular basket – 12–15 in (30–37.5 cm) diameter; loose-weave cream/beige hessian; coarse-gauge chicken wire – approx. 2 yds (1.8 m); stub/florists' wire – 3 packets long medium gauge; reel wire; old bricks; glue gun or cold glue; wire-cutters; scissors.

METHOD

Fill the basket with bricks or similar to weight the base of this arrangement, which is about 4 ft (1.2 m) high when finished.

Bend the chicken wire into a big, sturdy dome about 2 ft 6 in (75 cm) high and tie it firmly to the rim of the container with reel wire.

Wrap a strip of hessian round each of the 2 logs and tie it into a neat knot. Slip a length of reel wire through the hessian at the back and tie the logs next to each other on the frame.

Using reel wire, tie the bag of herbs to the frame centre right.

Ease a length of stub/florists' wire through the loaves and rolls to tie them to the dome at the front and sides in roughly the same positions as shown in the illustration opposite. Make sure the rim of the basket is hidden. The rolls and loaves will gradually dry out to become as hard as concrete.

Using a hot glue gun (preferably) or cold glue, attach stub/florists' wire to the base of each scallop shell and attach them together to the frame.

Divide the wheat into about 11 graded bunches, trim the stalks to about 2 in (5 cm) below the heads and wire the bunches with stub/florists' wire (see p. 19). Also wire some of the stalks into 3 or more even, fan-shaped bunches. Attach them all by their wire 'stems' to the frame.

The wild oats are trimmed and made into 7 graded and wired bunches, as above, and attached round the sides of the frame, sometimes next to the wheat.

Do not trim the golden yarrow before you make up 3 very uneven wired bunches to place round the top of the dome.

Very delicately attach the 2 birds' nests using reel wire.

Divide the remaining ingredients into at least the following number of loose, graded, wired clusters and add them to the arrangement in any order you wish: roses – 5; yellow *Helipterum sandfordii* – 5; pink sunray – 2; strawberry – 2 (1 large, 1 small); orange-tipped safflower – 2; dark red *Helichrysum* – 6 (4 on the left); orange-yellow *Helichrysum* – 2; lavender – 3; and marjoram – 2.

Bread in various shapes and hues combined with glorious flowers make a striking composition.

PARTERRE

INGREDIENTS

Tree branch – approx. 2 ft (60 cm) long, 2 in (5 cm) diameter

Ordinary green 'sack' moss (Mnium) – 1 large packet

Almost black, glycerine-dried magnolia leaves – approx. 400

Green sphagnum moss – 1 small packet

EQUIPMENT

Spherical basket – approx. 12 in (30 cm) diameter; dry-foam sphere (from florist) or make your own sphere (roll of fine-gauge chicken wire, 2–3 blocks of dry foam; see p. 16) – approx. 10 in (25 cm) diameter; plastic sheet – approx. 3 ft (90 cm) square; plaster of Paris or quick-drying cement – 1 medium packet; bucket and stirring implement; stub/florists' wire – 6 or more packets medium gauge; staple gun or reel wire (if using your own sphere); glue gun or cold glue; pliers; knife.

METHOD

Line the container with plastic so that nothing seeps through the basketwork and fill it almost to the brim with a thick mix of plaster or cement.

Swiftly rinse the bucket and stirrer to prevent them cracking.

Press the straight tree branch into the centre of the container until the end touches the bottom. Twist it several times so that the plaster or cement adheres and then hold or prop up the trunk until the mixture is set firm.

If you are using a shop-bought foam sphere, press it on to the top of the trunk so that the shape of the wood is indented in the foam. With a sharp knife cut out a hole smaller in diameter than the trunk and about 3 in (7.5 cm) deep. Cover the top of the trunk with glue and impale the foam ball firmly upon it. Cover the sphere with ordinary moss affixed with U-shaped pieces of stub/florists' wire.

If you are making your own moss-covered sphere, follow the instructions given on p. 16, but, instead of closing the chicken wire completely, leave a gap through which to insert the tree trunk. Wire or staple the foam-filled ball to the trunk and cover it with ordinary moss.

Thread a piece of stub/florists' wire through the bases of 2 or 3 magnolia leaves, one placed back to back with the others. Then twist the shorter wire end round the long one to tie the leaves together and insert the wire 'stem' in the ball. Do the same with the rest of the leaves. The leaves should stand at right angles to the surface. Use the pliers to bend the wire if your fingers become sore.

Green sphagnum moss is then glued in tight clumps round the base of the tree.

PRACTICAL HINT

To clean the leaves when they get dusty, wipe them with a slightly moist piece of cottonwool.

If you can find a plastic pot which will fit inside the basket, you could set the trunk in that instead, but then lifting the pliable basket may prove awkward. In any event, the tree base must be heavier than the top.

PARTERRE

No matter where it stands, this sleek, up-to-the-minute tree with its gleaming leaves looks superb and very stylish.

INGREDIENTS

Ordinary green 'sack' moss (Mnium) – 1 sack

Green beech leaves on branches (Fagus sylvatica) – 14 branches or more

Green oak leaves on branches (Quercus palustris) – 8 branches or more

Yellow Australian book leaves – 24 or more

Mexican white pine cones (Pinus ayacahuite) – 11 or more

Lemon yellow everlasting/strawflowers (Helichrysum bracteatum) – 6 bunches

Orange everlasting/strawflowers (Helichrysum bracteatum) – 6 bunches

Yellow yarrow (Achillea filipendulina) – 6 bunches

Yellow thistles (Cynara sp) – 9 stems

Yellow South African daisies/Lonas (Lonas inodora) or miniature yellow chrysanthemums (Chrysanthemum sp) – 10 bunches

White baby's breath (Gypsophila) – 6 bunches

White sago bush/Lachnostachys (Lachnostachys sp) – 6 bunches

Yellow kangaroo paw (Anigozanthos sp) – 6 bunches

Pink cardoon (Cynara sp) – 9 heads

Blue-green hydrangea (Hydrangea macrophylla) – 15 heads

Green love-lies-bleeding (Amaranthus caudatus 'Viridis') – 8 bunches

Yellow Stirlingia (Stirlingia latifolia) – 6 bunches

Pink-striped love-in-a-mist (Nigella damascena) – 4 bunches

EQUIPMENT

Large urn or similar; 1 yd- (90 cm-) wide coarse-gauge chicken wire – approx. 10 ft (3 m) long; sufficient bricks or similar to fill container to the rim; reel wire; canes – 20; stub/florists' wire – 2 packets long medium gauge, 2 packets long coarse gauge; wire-cutters; scissors.

METHOD

There are various ways of creating a base for this arrangement, but here is just one. Fill the container to the rim with old bricks or similar. On top of this you construct a dome. Unroll one end of the chicken wire over the bricks, pile moss high on top of it and then bend the remaining chicken wire back over the heap of moss. 'Stitch' the two ends of chicken wire together by running reel wire in and out of them. It now looks like a squashed roll. Firmly pack in more moss and gradually bend down the open sides of chicken wire until you have a dome. Using reel wire, attach the dome to the rim in whatever way seems most appropriate to the particular container.

If any ingredients are too short, extend the stalks with a cane (see p. 20) or with stub/florists' wire as you would when making a loose wired bunch (see pp. 19–20).

To create the basic shape, start by inserting the beech and oak branches, with some hanging down over the rim, followed by the yellow book leaves and wired cones (see p. 19).

Loosely wire the 12 bunches of *Helichrysum* (see p. 19) and scatter them all over the arrangement, some low down, some higher up.

All the other ingredients are then inserted, piece by piece, including the *Nigella* in 9 loosely wired bunches. There is no hard and fast order for doing this – use your judgement as to what looks best. Remember, though, that some heads should protrude further than others and some ingredients should only be glimpsed behind others, so that the finished arrangement has depth and looks as uncontrived as possible.

PRACTICAL HINT

If the budget is limited, increase the quantities of less expensive ingredients, but never scrimp on the amount you put in.

Large spaces require compositions on a grand scale, but by using smaller quantities the same arrangement would provide a splendid adornment to most homes.

Ingredients

Magnolia leaves – 40 or so

Red hybrid tea roses – 1 bunch

Cream everlasting/strawflowers (Helichrysum sp) – 2 bunches

Golden-green lady's mantle (Alchemilla mollis) – 2 bunches

Golden sage flowers (Phlomis) – 2 bunches

Marjoram (Origanum vulgare) – 3 bunches

Lavender (Lavendula spica) – 3 bunches

Wine red broom bloom (Gypsophila rugosa) – 1 bunch

Opium poppy seedheads (Papaver somniferum) – 22 small heads

Blue hydrangea (Hydrangea macrophylla) – 9 heads

Maroon peonies (Paeonia lactiflora) – 3 heads

Rose or other stalks – 5 or more bunches

Equipment

Piece of light, soft board approx. 2 ft (60 cm) × 7 in (17.5 cm) × ¹/₂ in (1.25 cm); dry foam – 2 blocks; chicken wire – approx. 2 ft (60 cm) fine gauge; cold glue; staple-gun or a hammer and metal U pins; stub/florists' wire – 2 packets medium gauge; ribbon; pliers; wire-cutters; scissors; long knife.

Method

Using a long, sharp knife such as a carving or bread knife, lay each foam block on its long side and slice it in half. Firmly glue the slices lengthways down the backing board and trim the corners on the long sides of the foam obliquely.

Lay the chicken wire over the foam and staple or nail it tightly to the board. Trim any protruding wire spikes on which you might cut yourself.

Wire the magnolia leaves in overlapping groups of twos and threes, leaving one end of stub/florists' wire protruding below by about 3 in (7.5 cm). The flowers are grouped on the plaque in four rough and unequal layers (see opposite), so insert about one third of the magnolia leaves in the foam round the top quarter of the plaque and gently bend them back so that they cover the edges of the board. Insert most of the rest of the leaves, leaving the occasional gap (see opposite) until you reach three-quarters of the way down the board. Keep back the few remaining leaves until after the two rows of stalks have been added.

Divide the dried flowers and seedheads into the following number of short, compact clusters and wire them (see p. 19): roses 3; *Helichrysum* 5; *Alchemilla mollis* 5 plus a couple of tiny ones; *Phlomis* 2; marjoram 7; lavender 5 or 7; broom bloom 4; and poppies 3. Leave wire stems approximately 3 in (7.5 cm) long.

Insert the flowers into the plaque from the top of the arrangement downwards. At the very top goes a cluster of lavender, on its left some

PARTERRE

The darkly mysterious frame of glycerine-dried magnolia leaves and the richly coloured flowers together evoke the glories of the Renaissance.

Alchemilla mollis, below that cream *Helichrysum*, in the centre red roses, on the right a blue hydrangea head, and so on down (see opposite below). Bear in mind the peonies.

Do not forget to cover the sides – keep checking from that angle – and remember that darker flowers like the marjoram and lavender may not show to best advantage against the almost black magnolia leaves, so put them in the gaps between the leaves.

Before putting on the last magnolia leaves and flower clusters, attach the 2 rows of stalks.

Using half the quantity of stalks, the bottom row is attached first. Trim a compact bunch of stalks to about 7 in (17.5 cm) long. Check that this is long enough by holding them against the foam – they should protrude about 3–4 in (7.5–10 cm) below the end of the board. Wire the bunch firmly at one end (see p. 19), leaving about 3 in (7.5 cm) wire extending beyond the stems, bend the wire over almost parallel to the stalks and push it downwards into the foam in the centre. Add the rest of the bunches, placing them close together, gradually fanning out each side.

The same process is followed for the top row of stalks, each bunch approximately 8 in (20–22.5 cm) long, their ends covering any remaining outline of the board.

Now you place the last few magnolia leaves on either side, to hide the stalk tops, and insert the remaining flower clusters to conceal the stalk wires. Finally attach a double bow of the best quality ribbon you can afford.

PRACTICAL HINT
Before starting to attach the clusters, it may prove helpful to lay out the ingredients beside the board in the order in which they appear in the photograph opposite, so that it is easier to work out which clusters go where down the sides.

INGREDIENTS
Lavender, preferably Hidcote Blue (Lavendula spica) – 20 bunches
Lavender, rose or other coarse stalks – 15–20 bunches

EQUIPMENT
Dry foam – 1 block; cork board, ½ in (1.25 cm) thick – approx. 12 in (30 cm) × 8 in (20 cm); cold glue; stub/florists' wire – 18–20 packets fine gauge; raffia – 1 shank; scissors; wire-cutters; knives.

METHOD
Using a sharp knife such as a retractable-blade Stanley knife, shape the cork into a rounded oval plaque about 12 in (30 cm) × 8 in (20 cm).

Lay the foam block on its long side and, with a long sharp knife (like a carving or bread knife), cut the block into 3 or more ¾ in (2 cm)-thick slices. On a flat, undamageable surface lay these slices long edge to long edge, one above the other, so that they form a rectangle of about 12 in (30 cm) × 8 in (20 cm). Without moving the foam, carefully lay the cork plaque on top and mark its outline on the foam. Trim the foam inside the outline so that it does not protrude and glue the foam firmly on to the plaque.

Make short, tight bunches of lavender, very slightly graded (see p. 19). Wire round each bunch just below the heads, trim the stalks and leave a wire 'stem' of about 3 in (7.5 cm). Beginning at the top edge of the plaque and then working down the sides, insert the bunches into the foam with their heads outwards protruding beyond the edge of the cork. If the wire penetrates the cork, so much the better.

Because the lavender head of the stook must be plump when finished, pack the lavender tightly together, overlapping the heads of each bunch as you work inwards and downwards. Fill between half and two-thirds of the plaque with lavender.

Holding a bunch of stalks with one end towards you, wrap the end nearest you with stub/florists' wire, but bend the long wire 'stem' back along the stalks. Using half the stalk bunches, insert the wire 'stems' downwards into the foam so that the stalk ends protrude about 2½ in (6.25 cm) beyond the edge of the plaque. Begin in the centre and work outwards to create a fan shape.

Make the top row of stalks in the same way, attaching the bunches just below the lavender and checking that the bottom ends of the bunches conceal the edge of the plaque. Trim the edges of both layers of stalks cleanly.

To make the raffia bow, imagine that this is a real round stook. Wrap the raffia right round the plaque, covering all the wires. Cross over the two lengths of raffia in the centre and staple the cross-over with a staple-gun or a U-shaped piece of stub/florists' wire so that it cannot slip. Now tie a generous bow – no need for a knot first – and spread the loops and ends of the bow. Wire it to the cross-over and into the foam. Cut through the raffia wrapping the plaque at the sides, bind the loose ends with wire and tuck them neatly behind the lavender and stalks.

PRACTICAL HINT
Attaching a hook to the back of the cork and hanging it on a length of chain is an attractive and adaptable way to hang one or more plaques. For a more elegant look, cover the chain with broad velvet ribbon.

PARTERRE

A traditional flower is presented in a lovely and original way in this plaque which looks like a plump stook of lavender.

INGREDIENTS
Lavender (Lavendula spica) – 8 bunches
Pale pink peonies (Paeonia lactiflora) – 6
Red hybrid tea roses – 2–3 bunches
Sphagnum moss – 1 packet

EQUIPMENT
Wall basket; dry foam – 2 blocks; stub/florists' wire – 1 packet medium gauge; wire-cutters; knife.

METHOD
Fill the container quite firmly with foam (see p. 15) and hang it on the wall. Using the medium-gauge stub/florists' wire, make graded bunches of lavender (see p. 19) with 12 or more heads, varying the number and lengths of the heads.

Trim the wire to leave at least 3 in (7.5 cm) below the stalks. Place the first bunch at the back, in the centre of the foam, leaning slightly. Insert other bunches round the back and sides, leaning left or right as appropriate, then work across the middle towards the front. Allow plenty of lavender to come out beyond the edge.

Now trim the peony stems so that the flower heads will nestle amongst the lavender and not protrude too far beyond the mass. Do not put any of them dead centre. Insert them carefully, gently parting the lavender with your free hand. Check from front and sides that the peonies are naturally spaced and that some face sideways.

Next, wire up the red rose heads (see p. 18) and trim to a length that will permit them to stand slightly above the mass of the lavender, so that the arrangement does not look too flat and compact. Space the roses around the basket, including the sides.

Check that any foam still visible at the edges is covered by lavender or small clumps of sphagnum moss pinned into the foam with 'hairpins' of stub/florists' wire.

ALEX MACCORMICK

Hanging a basket of flowers can be as pretty as a picture.

INGREDIENTS

Gum nuts – 100
Leucodendron (stem with series of 'arrows') – 3
 long pieces
Flat fungi – 9
Palm spears (Palmatus sp) – 34
Opium poppy seedheads (Papaver somniferum)
 – 13
Lotus flower (fruit) (Nelumbo lucifera) – 11
South African exotica like tightly curled rams'
 horns – 5
Protea repens flat – 3
South African exotica like a pair of curved deer
 horns – 6

EQUIPMENT

Damaged frame and mirror; gold paint (from artists' supplies shop) – 1 can; (optional) lavender matt paint; paint brushes – 1 medium, 1 small; glue gun.

METHOD

Paint the mirror frame gold and, if you wish, lavender. Try to choose a soft gold paint, so that the finished effect will not look too new and garish.

Whilst the paint is drying on the mirror frame, paint or spray all the ingredients gold. Do not worry if the finish is uneven – it will help give the illusion of age.

Once the paint on the frame and on the ingredients is completely dry, begin by glueing on the small gum nuts at intervals round the inside of the frame.

Cut the 3 pieces of *Leucodendron* into 9 pieces in total (1 piece will not be used).

In the centre of the top of the frame glue on 5 flat fungi overlapping in a fan shape, plus 1 either side of the 'fan'. Then attach about 5 palm spears, 5 or 6 poppy seedheads, 8 or so lotus flowers, 3 tightly curled 'rams' horns', 2 short pieces of *Leucodendron* and 1 *Protea repens* flat.

In the centre at the bottom of the frame place 3 palm spears, 1 poppy seedhead and 1 short piece of *Leucodendron*.

In the middle of either side glue 2 lotus flowers, 1 *Protea repens* flat and 2 pieces of *Leucodendron*.

At each bottom corner arrange 1 lotus flower, 1 tightly curled 'rams' horn', 1 poppy seedhead, 1 flat fungus and 2 pieces of *Leucodendron*.

The 6 pieces of exotica which resemble pairs of loosely curved deer horns are glued along the top of the frame.

All the remaining palm spears are attached to the frame on either side of the mirror and so too, at intervals, are the rest of the poppy seedheads.

PRACTICAL HINT

If some of the exotica are not easily available, seek substitutes with equally interesting shapes such as contorted willow, eucalyptus, cones, various kinds of nuts, pasta, shells, etc. – be inventive.

JULIET WILLIS

Restoring a gilt frame can be immensely costly when professionally done, but gold-painted dried plants offer an exciting, effective and inexpensive alternative.

FOODIE MIRROR FRAME

INGREDIENTS
Green spaghetti – 1 packet
White spaghetti – 1 packet
Cinnamon sticks – 8
Green and white tagliatelli 'balls' – 8
Pasta shells – ¹/₂ packet
*Amaretto biscuits wrapped in green, blue and
    pink paper – 4*
Baby bread rolls – 6
Wine corks – 12
*Nuts: hazel, brazil, almonds, pecans, walnuts –
    20 or more*
Garlic heads and cloves – 6
Artichokes (Cynara scolymus) – 3
*Lotus flower (fruit) (Nelumbo lucifera) – 6
    small, 3 large*
Flat fungi – 6
Golden mushrooms – 4
Brown seedpods – 4
Pink peppercorns on stalks – 1 packet
*Rattan palm/wait-a-while vine (Calamus sp) –
    1 large branch of mini 'cones'*
Artificial fruit – 7 red cherries, 3 crab apples

EQUIPMENT
Mirror with gilt frame – 2 ft (60 cm) overall
height, frame 3 in (7.5 cm) wide; glue gun
(preferably) or cold glue; raffia.

METHOD
Using under 1 packet of each, chop the white
and green spaghetti into 5 in (12.5 cm) lengths
and make 2 bundles of each colour tied neatly
with raffia.

The cinnamon sticks are cut into 3 in (7.5 cm)
lengths, 3 or 4 of which are then tied with raffia
into 4 small bundles.

In any order you wish, glue the ingredients
firmly to the frame with the nuts, corks, pasta
shells, cherries and clusters of pink peppercorns
punctuating the arrangement and covering any
small gaps.

PRACTICAL HINT
For a bathroom, substitute lots of different shells
in various sizes for the ingredients connected
with food.

JULIET WILLIS

A battered mirror frame takes on a new guise when imaginatively decorated with dried plants interspersed with ingredients from the kitchen store cupboard.

INGREDIENTS
Sphagnum moss – 1 packet
Pink hybrid tea roses – 3 bunches
Maroon hybrid tea roses – 3 bunches

EQUIPMENT
Dry-foam sphere – approx. 7 in (17.5 cm) diameter (home-made or from florist); green reel wire; stub/florists' wire – 1 packet medium gauge; reel of tough garden wire; silk or velvet ribbon – approx. 3 ft (90 cm); pliers; scissors; wire-cutters.

METHOD
If you wish to make your own moss-covered dry-foam sphere, follow the directions on p. 16. Do not forget to leave a small loop of binding wire at the top to thread the ribbon through.

If you have purchased a bare dry-foam sphere, cover it all over with clusters of sphagnum moss fixed into place with U-shaped 'hairpins' of stub/florists' wire.

Very delicately wire the rose heads (see p. 18), leaving approximately 3 in (7.5 cm) of wire to penetrate the foam. Rest the sphere on a table and, leaving a bare patch at the top and bottom, cover it with the rose heads, arranging them close to each other in groups and swirls (see opposite).

If your sphere is commercially produced, secure the ribbon to it by taking a length of long firm garden wire, bending it into a U shape and threading the ribbon under the U. Stick the wire ends through the top of the sphere, push them right through to the bottom, and then bend the ends upwards and back into the foam so that it is firmly fixed in place.

If your sphere is home-made, simply thread the ribbon through the binding-wire loop.

Now you can hang up the sphere and finish covering it with roses. Then tie the ribbon into a pretty bow and slide the ribbon round until the bow is above the flowers.

PRACTICAL HINT
For fragrance add a few drops of essential rose oil to the foam sphere or on to the flowers.

ALEX MACCORMICK

With its swirls of pink and maroon, this rose ball has the same well-crafted,

timeless appeal as a novel by Jane Austen.

INGREDIENTS
(Clockwise from left)
(1) Purple statice (Limonium sinuatum) – 1 piece
  Pinky mauve statice (Limonium sinuatum) – 1 piece
  Mauve miniature globe thistle (Echinops ritro) – 2 heads
  Lavender (Lavendula spica) – 3 heads
  Green-grey oregano (Origanum sp) – 1 piece
  Dark red love-lies-bleeding (Amaranthus sp) – 1 head
(2) Green Ruscus – 5 small pieces
(3) Pink broom bloom (Gypsophila rugosa) – 1 cluster
  White Bupleurum (Bupleurum sp) – 2 small clusters
  Golden brown grass (Gramina) – 1 cluster
  Wine red everlasting/strawflowers (Helichrysum bracteatum) – 3 small flowers
  Yellow feather flower (Verticordia sp) – 1 small piece
(4) Salmon pink miniature sunray (Helipterum sp) – 1 small bunch
(5) Pink everlasting/strawflowers (Helichrysum bracteatum) – 5 flowers
  Pinky mauve statice (Limonium sinuatum) – 1 piece
  Pinky orange Dudinea (Dudinea sp) – 1 head
  Pink delphinium (Delphinium sp) – 6 tips of heads
  Love-in-a-mist (Nigella damascena) – 2 small heads
  Golden yarrow (Achillea sp) – 1 small head
  Green sphagnum moss – 1 handful

EQUIPMENT
(1) Old brass egg cup approx 2 in (5 cm) high; (2) crystal vase approx. 4 in (10 cm) high; (3) blue glass vase 2 in (5 cm) high; (4) silver salt cellar 2 in (5 cm) long, 1^1/$_4$ in (3 cm) high; (5) crystal salt cellar 3 in (7.5 cm) long, 1^3/$_4$ (4 cm) high; dry foam – 1 block; adhesive clay; scissors; knife.

METHOD
(1) Sculpt some dry foam into a tiny ball to fit the egg cup and fix it in place with adhesive clay. Trim the flowers as necessary and press their stalks gently into the foam.
(2) Trim the green *Ruscus*, if necessary, and arrange it.
(3) First insert the cluster of broom bloom and the 2 clusters of white *Bupleurum*, followed by the golden brown grass. No need to wire them, but trim them if necessary. The red *Helichrysum* and yellow feather flower are tucked in round the rim.
(4) Shape a piece of foam to fit the silver salt cellar and fix it in place with adhesive clay. Trim the stalks of the sunray and insert them into the foam in small fingerfuls. Add extra loose heads, if necessary, to fill any gaps.
(5) Sculpt a piece of dry foam to fix in the centre of the glass salt cellar with adhesive clay, conceal the sides of the foam with moss and insert the flower stalks into the foam after trimming.

PRACTICAL HINT
Handle the *Ruscus* with care and keep it away from small children because it is sharp and spiky.

ALEX MACCORMICK

Miniature arrangements exert a powerful fascination, are ideal for gifts or decorating individual places at a dining table, and look captivating in groups.

ALEX MACCORMICK

INGREDIENTS
Pink roses – 1¹/₂ –2 bunches
White roses – 1¹/₂ –2 bunches
Sphagnum moss – 1 small packet

EQUIPMENT
Terracotta clay pot – approx. 6 in (15 cm) diameter; dry foam – 1 block; stub/florists' wire – 1 packet medium gauge; wire-cutters; pliers; knife.

METHOD
Shape the foam so that it fills the clay pot.

Carefully wire the rose heads (see p. 18), leaving approximately 3 in (7.5 cm) wire at the bottom. Insert the first 3 pink roses in the centre of the pot so that the heads stand about 2 in (5 cm) above the foam. The rest of the pink roses are positioned in tight swirls round the pot, like thick cream when it is first poured into a cup of black coffee. You are trying to create a shallow dome, so set the rose heads lower towards the edge until the ones at the rim almost touch it.

Then fill the gaps with the white roses close enough together to hide the dry foam, following the dome-shaped contour.

Finally, using 'hairpins' of stub/florists' wire, pop in bunches of sphagnum moss around the rim, allowing it to hang over the edge to soften the effect.

PRACTICAL HINT
If the rose pot is for a bedroom or lavatory, you might like to add a few drops of essential rose oil to it.

Two pots, one at each end, look particularly pretty on a bedroom mantelpiece or dressing table.

JEANETTE COLLINS

Whether on a side table or mantelpiece, easy-to-make pots of flowers can suit

your mood – charming or funny.

INGREDIENTS

Silver dollar gum (Eucalyptus cinerea) – 1–2 bunches

Golden poppy seedheads (Papaver gigantum) – 3 large

Spiky green love-in-a-mist (Nigella orientalis) – 1 bunch

Green love-lies-bleeding (Amaranthus caudatus 'Viridis') – 1 bunch

Red love-lies-bleeding (Amaranthus sp) – ¹/₂ bunch

Grey-green oregano (Origanum sp) – 1 bunch

Green Lepidium (Lepidium ruderale) – 1 bunch

Red-dyed safflower/dyer's saffron (Carthamus tinctorius) – 1 bunch

Yellow sunflower (Helianthus sp) – 4 heads

Crimson floribunda roses – 1 bunch

Yellow hybrid tea roses – 1 bunch

Golden yarrow (Achillea filipendulina) – 4 pieces

Deep pink artificial roses – 3

Peach artificial peonies – 6 open, 3 buds

Pink peonies (Paeonia lactiflora) – 9 flowers

Globe artichoke (Cynara scolymus) – 1 in flower, 1 not

EQUIPMENT

Oval basket – approx. 10 in (25 cm) long; building brick or similar; dry foam – 1–2 blocks; adhesive tape; stub/florists' wire – 1 packet long medium gauge; (optional) canes – 11; (optional) gutta-percha tape; wire-cutters; scissors; knife.

METHOD

Put a brick or similar in the basket to weight the base so that the arrangement will not topple over due to being top heavy.

On top of the brick, place 1 or more blocks of dry foam shaped to fit the basket and stand proud of the rim by at least 1 in (2.5 cm). Fix the dry foam in place with adhesive tape (see p. 15).

Place the eucalyptus at the back of the basket in a fan shape.

Attach the poppy seedheads, if necessary, to canes with wire (see p. 20) and bind the 'stems' in gutta-percha. Insert them toward the back.

Divide the following ingredients into about the number of graded wired bunches (see p. 19) specified, leaving long wire 'stems': *Nigella* – 4 (remove the leaves first); green *Amaranthus* – 5; red *Amaranthus* – 3; oregano – 5; and *Lepidium* – 7.

Insert the wired bunches in groups and drifts as they appear in the illustration opposite.

If the safflower, sunflower and crimson and yellow rose stalks are too short, wire each stalk as you would a bunch. Otherwise, they can be inserted directly into the arrangement, along with the golden yarrow and the artificial flowers.

Make sure that the arrangement looks good from the sides as well as from the front.

If the 9 peony and 2 artichoke heads are not already on canes or wired then you should wire them to canes (see p. 20) and cover them in gutta-percha before placing them in the basket.

PRACTICAL HINT

If possible, it is always best to make this arrangement actually in the fireplace instead of on a work top because then the proportion and balance are easier to assess and correct.

You may prefer to splash out on freeze-dried flowers instead of using artificial ones.

JEANETTE COLLINS

The lyrical colours of spring and early summer bring garden freshness to

a fireplace when it is not in use.

INGREDIENTS
Pink eucalyptus baby (Eucalyptus sp) – 3 bunches
Orange-tipped safflower/dyer's saffron
(Carthamus tinctorius) – 3 bunches
Bearded wheat (Triticum) – 2 bunches
Yellow everlasting/strawflower (Helichrysum
sp) – 3 bunches
White large-flowered sunray (Helipterum/
Rhodanthe sp) – 3 bunches

EQUIPMENT
Horn-shaped basket; dry foam – 1–1½ blocks; adhesive tape; reel wire; newspaper; stub/florists' wire – 2 packets long, medium gauge; beige gutta-percha tape; scissors; wire-cutters; knife.

METHOD
Fill the horn-shaped basket with crumpled newspaper (or similar) to within about 1 in (2.5 cm) of the rim of the basket, providing a firm base for the dry foam.

Shape the dry foam to fit the mouth of the basket and sculpt it into a prominent mound to extend as far as possible beyond the rim. Tape it firmly in place (see p. 15).

Insert the pointed horn into the chimney and rest the rim of the basket on the front of the fire grate or on the back of the fire basket. Secure it in place with reel wire.

Since you are creating what is, in effect, an upside-down fan shape, bear in mind that in the top one quarter to one third of the arrangement the plants should point upwards and then, gradually, towards you, the rest pointing downwards. The flowers should look as though they are pouring out of the horn.

Begin by inserting three-quarters of the pink eucalyptus round the edges of the arrangement to create an outline. Use shorter pieces at the top and longer ones lower down. Extend the stalks, if necessary, by winding a piece of stub/florists' wire round the end and leaving the long end of wire as an extension 'stem', much as you would for a bunch of flowers (see p. 19). If this is not long enough, add on another length of wire by twisting the two ends of the wires round each other.

The safflowers are placed next, with shorter pieces at the top and upper sides, longer ones towards the bottom. Also insert some shorter pieces in the central area pointing out towards you. Extend the safflower stalks, if necessary, as above.

Insert the remaining eucalyptus around the middle of the arrangement at various angles.

Now insert the wheat – mostly in twos and threes (wired together with stub/florists' wire, if necessary, as on pp. 19–20) – first of all around the edge to punctuate the safflower and eucalyptus, and then in the central area. Extend the stalks of the wheat which goes lower down by the same method as the eucalyptus above.

Wire the individual heads of *Helichrysum* and sunray (see p. 18). Then, using one or more pieces of stub/florists' wire taped end to end to extend the 'stems' (see p. 20), wire the flowers in clusters of 2, 3, 4 or 5 (see pp. 19–20). Place the clusters as you see them in the illustration opposite, adjusting them to cover any obvious gaps.

PRACTICAL HINT
If a block of dry foam is tied with reel wire to the back of the fire basket or to the grate below the wicker basket, the lower plants can be inserted into that, thus necessitating fewer very long wire 'stem' extensions and saving time.

Sparkling sunshine seems to fill an empty fireplace as flowers pour forth from a horn-shaped basket, thus solving a perennial problem.

INGREDIENTS (For 2)
Straight wooden branch or stick – 2, 4 ft (1.2 m)
long, 1/2 in (1.3 cm) diameter
Ordinary green 'sack' moss (Mnium) – 1 large
packet
Green reindeer moss (Cladonia rangiferina) – 1
large packet

EQUIPMENT
2 terracotta clay flowerpots – 6 in (15 cm) diameter; fine-gauge chicken wire; plaster of Paris – 1 packet and 1/2 block of dry foam, or quick-drying cement – 1 packet; stub/florists' wire – 2 packets fine gauge; reel wire; mixing bowl and stirrer; glue gun or cold glue; wire-cutters; scissors; knife.

METHOD
The same method applies to both trees.

If you are using plaster, line the pot with slices of dry foam to prevent it from cracking. Make a thick, creamy mix of plaster or cement and fill three-quarters of the pot.

Speedily rinse clean the mixing bowl and stirring implement before the mixture sets on them.

Tap the base of the pot to settle the mixture and insert a branch or stick to form the tree trunk. Twist the trunk to coat it and either prop it up or hold it vertical until the base has set hard.

The length of chicken wire needed is difficult to gauge, but it will probably be just over 3 ft 6 in (1.05 m) long. It does not matter, however, if it is too long. Place ordinary moss along the smooth edge of the chicken wire and roll it over to form a long sausage about 2 1/2 in (6.5 cm) in

diameter, slightly thinner at what will be the top end. Cut off the surplus width of chicken wire and then 'stitch' the two long edges together by running reel wire in and out along the length. Leave a length of at least 7 in (17.5 cm) open at the top end. Make sure that the entire length of the 'sausage' is packed with moss and bend into it any protruding spikes of chicken wire.

Using short pieces of U-shaped stub/florists' wire, cover the 'sausage' with small clumps of reindeer moss up to the open section. Do not worry if the moss varies in shade – it looks more natural. Tie the bottom of the 'sausage' firmly to the 'tree trunk' with reel wire and then wind the 'sausage' round the trunk to within about 7 in (17.5 cm) of its top. Wrap the open section of 'sausage' round the top of the trunk so that it forms a narrowing point into which the trunk seems to disappear. 'Stitch' together the chicken wire with reel wire and cover it with reindeer moss as before.

Check that the shape looks pleasing and then, with sharp scissors, painstakingly trim the moss into a smooth outline.

To complete the base, glue reindeer moss to the surface of the plaster or cement.

PRACTICAL HINT
Reindeer moss is dyed a number of colours, so you do not have to stick to green.

An alternative method of making a spiral tree is to insert the 'trunk' into the closed top 7 in (17.5 cm) of the moss-filled 'sausage', wind the 'sausage' down the 'trunk', tie them together and set the bottom of both in the plaster or cement.

JULIET WILLIS

Why spend the earth buying live spiral trees which may at any moment die when you

can have virtually everlasting ones for well under half the price?

INGREDIENTS (For 2)
Silver birch twigs (Betula pendula) – 1–2 bunches
Two varieties of small, bronze-leaved eucalyptus
(Eucalyptus sp) – 4 bunches
Pale mauve flowering heather (Erica sp) – 2
bunches
Pale yellow rose buds – 12

EQUIPMENT
2 vases – approx. 7 in (17.5 cm) high, 3 in (7.5 cm) diameter at neck; 1 ft- (30 cm-) wide fine-gauge chicken wire; stub/florists' wire – 1 packet medium gauge; gold spray paint; wire cutters; scissors.

METHOD
Spray the silver birch twigs, each of which should be about 1 ft (30 cm) long, with gold paint and put them aside to dry.

Mould a length of chicken wire into a ball shape to fill the first vase, and do the same for the second vase.

To create the basic shape, make up loosely wired bunches containing 3 or 4 pieces of eucalyptus, each about 10 in (25 cm) long (see p. 19).

Insert them first of all in a fan shape at the back of the vases. As you work towards the front, the bunches lean sideways and forwards. Bend the wire 'stems' on some so that they fall over the rims and drape a few over the back if there is any chance of their being seen from that angle.

The golden twigs are then distributed at varying angles round the vases.

Using 2–3 pieces at a time, make the heather into loosely wired bunches and place them in the arrangement, scattered as you think best.

Finally, add 6 yellow roses to each vase. They should not need wiring, but, if you wish to do so, follow the instructions for wiring *Helichrysum* heads given on p. 18 rather than the usual method of wiring rose heads.

PRACTICAL HINT
By dividing the ingredients into separate piles for each vase before you start wiring and inserting them, the distribution of ingredients will look more even in the finished arrangements.

If dry foam is used instead of chicken wire inside the vases, the arrangements tend to look more rigid.

JULIET WILLIS

Because they include subtle bronze leaves and golden twigs, these arrangements complement their surroundings instead of competing with them.

INGREDIENTS

(All the ingredients should be as long as possible)

Contorted willow (Salix sp) – 2 or more large pieces

Long-eared bearded wheat (Triticum sp) – 2 bunches with leaves

Bamboo (Arundinaria sp) – approx. 11

Palm leaves (Palmatus sp) – 2 'fans'

Yellow Stirlingia (Stirlingia latifolia) – approx. 12 pieces

Red kangaroo paw (Anigozanthos rufus) – approx. 10 pieces

Wild oats (Avena fatua) – 2 bunches

White sea lavender (Limonium sp) – 2–3 bunches

EQUIPMENT

Container – approx. 2 ft (60 cm) high; coarse-gauge chicken wire; stub/florists' wire – 2 packets long medium gauge and 1 packet long coarse gauge or 28 poker wires 2 ft 6in (45 cm) long; 6 canes – approx. 4 ft (1.3m) long; beige, brown and pale green gutta-percha tape; adhesive tape; wire-cutters; scissors.

METHOD

Fill the container with chicken wire crumpled into a rough oval.

Arrange the contorted willow towards the back of the container, if it is to stand against a wall or in a corner; otherwise put it in the centre.

Using just under one third of the bearded wheat, wire up a graded bunch (see p. 19) tied towards the bottom of the stalks with medium-gauge stub/florists' wire, leaving a long wire 'stem'. This bunch appears high up amongst the contorted willow, so either fix the bunch by firmly winding the stub/florists' wire 'stem' round the main willow branch, or insert a long piece of poker wire or cane into the bunch and bind from the bunch to the bottom of this new 'stem' with pale-green gutta-percha (see p. 19).

Insert the bamboo at varying heights around the vase, keeping 1 short piece aside for later. Depending on the length and diameter of the bamboo canes, extend them (see p. 20) with poker wire, canes or joined pieces of coarse-gauge stub/florists' wire, bound in gutta-percha.

Wind a piece of medium-gauge wire round each of the 2 palm leaf stalks, leaving a long wire 'stem' (see pp. 19–20). Bend the wire 'stems' to angle the leaves over the edge of the vase and tape the 'stems' to the inside of the container.

Most of the pieces of yellow *Stirlingia*, which appear at various heights, will need lengthening either with poker wire or with several pieces of stub/florists' wire joined together (see p. 20). The wire 'stem' is then bound to the plant stalk with brown gutta-percha, all the way down. Keep a few short pieces of *Stirlingia* for later.

Then the red kangaroo paw is dispersed around the arrangement. Extend the stalks as necessary using the same method as for the *Stirlingia* above. Save a few short pieces for later.

The wild oats are made into four graded and wired bunches (see p. 19), and an extension 'stem' is added using poker wire or a cane, which is then bound in beige gutta-percha. 2 bunches are placed to the right-hand side, 2 to the left.

The remainder of the wheat is divided into 3 graded, wired bunches as for the first bunch. An extension 'stem' is added using the same method as for the wild oats. One bunch should have a 'stem' about 9 in (22.5 cm) longer than the other 2; this bunch is inserted just right of centre to conceal the bottom of the first wheat bunch high up in the willow. The remaining 2 bunches are placed left of centre and encouraged to spread.

Round the lower part of the arrangement insert any short pieces of kangaroo paw, bamboo and *Stirlingia*, and all of the sea lavender.

Check the arrangement from all angles, adjusting the plants where necessary.

Although this inspired composition looks marvellous in a large space, it also adds

drama to a corner in a smaller room.

Whiter shades of pale – tropical sun and sea are echoed here with cool

sophistication and exotic touches.

INGREDIENTS

Stirlingia bud (Stirlingia latifolia) – 1 bunch not in flower

Bleached fescue grass (Festuca sp) or bleached reeds (Phragmitis australis) – 7 stems

Bleached contorted willow (Salix sp) – 1 bunch

Bleached palm leaf (Palmatus sp) – 2 'fans'

Bleached leaves 6 or 7, any long leaved variety e.g. Australian book leaves

White sea lavender (Limonium sp) – 2 bunches

Bleached fern (Dryopteris sp) – 2 bunches

Honesty (Lunaria rediviva) – 1 bunch

Onion (Allium sp) – 1 bunch

South Australian daisy (Ixodia sp) – 2–3 bunches

White botao/common camomile (Anthemis nobilis) – 2 bunches

Sandplain woody pear (Xylomelum angustifolium) – 1 branch

Bleached hare's/pussy tail grass (Lagurus ovatus) – 1 bunch

Trichinium australis or clematis seedheads (Clematis sp) – 4

Reindeer moss (Cladonia rangiferina) – 1 small packet

EQUIPMENT

Large seashell; dry foam – 1–1½ blocks; florists' spikes – 2 or more; adhesive clay; stub/florists' wire – 1 packet medium gauge; scissors; knife; wire-cutters.

METHOD

Fix the dry foam firmly to the shell by impaling it on florists' spikes attached to the shell with adhesive clay.

Insert the wiry, dark *Stirlingia* right round the back of the shell.

To create the outline of the basic fan shape of this arrangement, place the individual *Festuca* or *Phragmitis* and contorted willow at various angles across the back of the foam, some leaning slightly forwards, others slightly back. Place 1 piece of contorted willow left of centre in the middle of the foam or slightly towards the front.

Wrap one end of a piece of stub/florists' wire round the base of the largest palm 'fan', leaving at least 4 in (10 cm) of wire 'stem' at the bottom. Press this firmly into the foam on the left-hand side and twist the 'fan' so that it faces towards you and drapes over the side of the shell. Wire the other 'fan' and place it on the right-hand side further back than the first one.

Add any odd long bleached leaves across the middle and towards the back, wiring them first, if necessary, as you did the palm.

Next put the longer pieces of sea lavender behind, between and in front of the grass/reeds, leaves and contorted willow; use the shorter pieces in the middle of the shell with a few towards the front. The sea lavender should create a haze as though you had draped a fine-mesh fishing net through the arrangement.

Place most of the white fern on the right-hand side towards the middle and front, and delicately insert the other fronds amongst the sea lavender in the centre and back left.

4 or 5 of the tallest honesty are then spread across the middle of the arrangement; any smaller pieces can be inserted later towards the front.

Add the creamy-gold onion flower heads at varying heights towards the back, 1 each side leaning forwards and a rather shorter one left of centre in the middle also leaning towards you.

Scatter stems of South Australian daisy across the middle and group shorter, trimmed and wired bunches (see p. 19) at the front.

White botao are placed individually or in twos and threes from the middle to the front, with some amongst the bunches of daisies.

The woody pear branch then goes in the middle, its stalk wired as for a bunch (see p. 19), leaning right beneath the shortest *Allium*.

The oval furry *Lagurus* grass is spread out across the middle with some leaning left and right as well as towards the front, generally above the tops of the daisies.

Any dry foam still visible is covered by reindeer moss attached by 'hairpins' of stub/florists' wire.

Finally the delicate, rich cream mopheads of *Trichinium* or clematis are placed on a rising diagonal from lower front right to centre left.

INGREDIENTS
Tree branch – 24 in (60 cm) long, 2 in (5 cm)
  diameter
Hoja leaves – 16
Flat moss (Mnium sp)   1 large piece
Red flat fungi – 4
Lotus flower (fruit) (Nelumbo lucifera) – 3 large
Sea shells – 15 various
Golden mushrooms – 9

EQUIPMENT
Terracotta clay pot – approx. 6 in (15 cm) diameter; 1 packet plaster of Paris and ½ block of dry foam, or 1 packet quick-drying cement; mixing bowl and stirring implement; stub/florists' wire – 1 packet long, medium gauge; chicken wire – any gauge; staple gun; glue gun; cold glue; bronze spray paint; matt black spray paint; dark blue spray paint; verdigris spray paint; small sponge; wire-cutters; scissors.

METHOD
Line the pot with slices of dry foam to prevent it cracking if you are using plaster. (Plaster expands as it dries.) Make a thick mix of plaster or cement and fill the pot to within 1 in (2.5 cm) of the rim. Wash out the mixing bowl and stirrer as soon as you have finished with them.

Tap the bottom of the clay pot a couple of times on the work surface to get rid of any air bubbles and insert the tree trunk. Twist it back and forth to cover it in cement or plaster, then hold it vertical until the base has set hard.

Meanwhile cover the Hoja leaves with bronze spray paint. When that is dry, spray on black, blue or a little verdigris and then wipe some of it off with the sponge. Also try dabbing on extra layers of paint using the sponge. The leaves should look as though they are made of weathered metal.

Mould the chicken wire into a distorted mushroom head and staple it to the top of the tree trunk. Cover the chicken wire by glueing pieces of flat moss on to it.

Wind one end of a piece of stub/florists' wire round the bases of the red fungi as you would a loose bunch (see pp. 19–20) or glue the wire to the fungi. Insert the long wire 'stems' through the moss until they protrude the other side of the tree head, and then bend the wire end back into the moss to hold the fungi firmly at varying angles.

Attach the lotus flowers using the same method.

Alternately attach the painted Hoja leaves in the same manner as the lotus flowers and glue in place the shells and small golden mushrooms.

Smear some paint over the terracotta clay pot to tone it down and cover the base round the tree trunk with moss affixed with cold glue.

PRACTICAL HINT
Although hot glue from a glue gun does not work on every surface, it saves a great deal of time on most arrangements because it dries so quickly.

This weird and wonderful tree with its unusual hues and textures seems to have come from some strange imaginary land.

INGREDIENTS
Tree bark – enough strips to cover the base
Green brome (Bromus sp)/Isolepsis – 2–3 bunches
Lotus flower (fruit) (Nelumbo lucifera) – 15 large
Aerial roots of Mauritius nuts – 6–7 clumps
Mauritius nuts (with and without stalks) – 13
Birds' eggs – 24
Grey Spanish moss – 1 packet

EQUIPMENT
Large plastic bucket; coarse-gauge chicken wire – approx. 1 yd (90 cm) square; fine-gauge brown reel wire; glue gun (preferably) or cold glue; raffia; wire-cutters; scissors.

METHOD
Wrap the chicken wire round the bucket and tie it with reel wire. Then mould the chicken wire above the bucket into a dome shape.

Tie the strips of bark tightly to the chicken wire round the bucket with reel wire. If the wire is tight enough, it will dig into the bark and not be too obvious. Trim the knotted reel wire ends neatly. Overlap the edges of some strips of bark, but do not worry if there are a few gaps because these can be hidden later.

Divide the green brome into 10, tie a length of raffia round the bottom of each bunch and then bind them by spiralling the raffia up the bunches from the bottom to the top. Bend the brome into the shape you want as you bind – it will droop naturally anyway. Tie the raffia in a knot at the top to secure the binding.

Push the ends of the brome bunches through the chicken-wire dome, and twist and turn them to achieve the desired effect.

Beginning at the bottom and working upwards, tie the lotus flowers to the chicken wire using reel wire. Do this over a gap, where there is a shorter strip of bark or on to the wire dome as you approach the top.

Check the arrangement regularly from every angle unless it is going to stand against a wall or in a corner.

The aerial roots, which come in clumps, are also attached by reel wire to the chicken-wire frame wherever you can see it between the bark. They can also be tied to the bark.

The shiny Mauritius nuts are glued to the bark and to their aerial roots or, if they have stalks, tie them to the chicken wire with reel wire.

Check that there are no wire ends which need trimming.

The fragile birds' eggs are glued to the lotus flowers and to the aerial roots.

To cover any remaining gaps, loose handfuls of Spanish moss are glued in place.

Shapes from fantasy

and fairy tale –

what can you dream up?

PARTERRE

SUPPLIERS OF DRIED FLOWERS AND ARRANGEMENTS

There are now thousands of dried flower stockists all over the world, but below are listed a few suggestions of some in Great Britain. To find others close to you, look in the *Yellow Pages* directory under 'Florists' and 'Florists' Supplies'. It is also worthwhile checking your local garden centre.

* Suppliers marked with this symbol have arrangements featured in this book.

† These suppliers also offer courses in arranging.

Branches of:
Boots, Habitat, Homebase, Lewis's, Makro, National Trust, Next

IN LONDON:
Covent Garden Flower Market,
New Covent Garden (Nine Elms),
London SW8 5NX.
Tel: 071–720–2211 (Visit before 8 am)

Chattels,
53 Chalk Farm Road, London
NW1 8AN.
Tel: 071–267–0877

Hillier & Hilton,
98 Church Road, London SW13 0DQ.
Tel: 081–748–1810

* † Juliet Willis,
336 Old York Road, London
SW18 1SS.
Tel: 081–874–9944

Kenneth Turner Flowers,
35 Brook Street, London W1Y 6BN.
Tel: 071–355–3880

* Mark Stacey (Freelance),
16 Avondale Road, London
SW19 8JX.
Tel: 081–542–6895

* McQueen's,
11 Great Eastern Street, London
EC2A 3ET.
Tel: 071–929–3078

* Parterre Flowers Ltd,
8 Marylebone Passage, London
W1N 7HE.
Tel: 071–323–1623
and London Marriott Hotel,
Grosvenor Square, London
W1A 4AW. Tel: 071–493–1232
(Arrangements only)

Patio,
155 Battersea Park Road, London
SW8 4BU.
Tel: 071–622–8262

Robert Day Flowers,
89 Pimlico Road, London
SW1 W8PH.
Tel: 071–824–8655

* Woodhams,
60 Ledbury Road, London W11 2AJ.
Tel: 071–243–3141

ENGLAND
* Aromaround,
64 High Street, Epping, Essex
CM16 4BP.
Tel: 0378–72102

† Country Flair,
Pooty Pools Farm, Radley Green
Road, Roxwell, Chelmsford, Essex
CM1 4NW. Tel: 0245–248425

The Hop Shop,
Castle Farm, Shoreham, Kent
TN14 7UB.
Tel: 09592–3219

Round House Flowers,
The Round House, Park Hatch,
Loxhill, Godalming, Surrey GU8 4BL.
Tel: 0483–200375

† Sussex Dried Flowers,
The Flower Barn, 37 Hill Lane,
Barnham, West Sussex P022 0BL.
Tel: 0243–553490

Park Place Flowers,
The Old Dairy, Park Place Farm,
Wickham, Fareham, Hants
P017 5HB. Tel: 0329–833808

Three Fs Everjoy,
Mantree Road, Shillingford St George,
Exeter, Devon EX2 9QR.
Tel: 0392–832218

Elmtree Dried Flowers,
Elmtree Farm, Frocester,
Nr Stonehouse, Glos
GL10 3TG. Tel: 0453–823274

Armscote Manor Dried Flowers,
Armscote, Nr Stratford-upon-Avon,
Warwickshire CV37 8DA.
Tel: 060882–681

Badger Bloomers,
Tyte Cottage, Ackleton,
Wolverhampton WV6 7JH.
Tel: 0746–5678

† Excelsior Dried Flowers,
37 Shirrall Drive, Drayton Bassett,
Tamworth, Staffs B78 3EQ.
Tel: 021–308–1329

Daisy Chain,
58 Street Lane, Roundhay, Leeds
LS8 2PQ. Tel: 0532–663039

Campion,
26 High Street, Uppermill, Oldham,
Lancs OL3 6HX.
Tel: 0457–876341

The Firth Partnership,
Rigglands, Blencarn, Penrith, Cumbria
CA10 1TX. Tel: 0768–88705

Barkers,
198–202 High Street, Northallerton,
North Yorkshire DL7 8LP.
Tel: 0609–772303

† Flowers Forever,
Brant Road, Fulbeck, Grantham, Lincs
NG32 3JZ. Tel: 0400–73275

† Country House Flowers,
Washingford House, Bergh Apton,
Norwich, Norfolk NR15 1AA.
Tel: 09085–0469

Bunches 'n' Bows,
Fen Nursery, Hacheston,
Woodbridge, Suffolk
IP13 9NB. Tel: 0728–724589

SCOTLAND
Casa Fina,
107 Hanover Street, Edinburgh
EH1 2DJ. Tel: 031–225–2422

Nova,
20 Chapel Street, Aberdeen AB1 1SP.
Tel: 0224–641270

Everlastings (Scottish Flowers),
Carnbee, Anstruther, Fife KY10 2RU.
Tel: 03338–318

WALES
Barkways,
245 Cathedral Road, Cardiff CF1 9TT.
Tel: 0222–397717

Clouds of Swansea,
Unit 8, St David's Centre, Swansea
SA1 3LE. Tel: 0792–648093

NORTHERN IRELAND
Trevor Edwards Garden Centre,
Scotch Quarter, Carrickfergus, Co.
Antrim BT38 DP. Tel: 09603–51123

Dixon & Co.,
Church Street, Coleraine BT52 1A4.
Tel: 0265–42076

INDEX

Achillea sp, 8; *Achillea filipendulina*, 32, 43, 56, 76, 100, 104, 108, 122, 126; *Achillea ptarmica*, 66
Actinidia vine, 18, 38, 46
Agonis juniperina, 24, 92
Aira sp, 30
Alchemilla mollis, 8, 32, 99, 110
Allium, 8, 137
Amaranthus sp, 59, 94, 122, 126; *Amaranthus caudatus 'Viridis'*, 82, 84, 108, 126
Anaphalis, 70
Anemone, 10
Anigozanthos sp, 108; *Anigozanthos rufus*, 134
Anthemis nobilis, 22, 137
Artichokes, globe (*Cynara scolymus*), 8, 32, 118, 126
Arundinaria sp, 96, 134
Australian book leaves, 108, 137
Avena fatua, 26, 104, 134

Baby's breath (*Gypsophila*), 24, 59, 82, 108
Bamboo leaves (*Arundinaria* sp), 96, 134
Bamboos, drying, 8
Barley (*Hordeum* sp), 26
Baskets, arrangements using, 26, 56, 60, 62, 65, 66, 72, 115
Bay leaves, 49
Beech leaves (*Fagus sylvatica*), 108; *see also* Copper Beech
Bells of Ireland (*Molucella*), 9
Betula pendula, 100, 132
Birch, green (*Fagus sylvatica*), 24; silver (*Betula pendula*), 100, 132
Botao/common camomile (*Anthemis nobilis*), 22, 137
Branch circle, 18
Branches, 46, 89, 90, 131
Brome (*Bromus* sp), 140
Broom bloom (*Gypsophila rugosa*), 26, 56, 81, 110, 122
Bulrushes, 8
Bupleurum (*Bupleurum* sp), 24, 122

Cacalia sp, 82
Calamus sp, 34, 118
Camomile, common, *see* Botao
Canary grass seedheads (*Phalaris* sp), 82
Cape honey flower (*Protea compacta*), 76
Cardoon (*Cynara* sp), 108
Carlina acaulis, 8, 78
Carthamus sp, 36, 66; *Carthamus tinctorius*, 76, 99, 104, 126, 128
Celosia cockscomb (*Celosia argentea cristata*), 28, 76
Centaurea cyranus, 10
Chenopodium, 8
Chilli peppers, 38
Chinese lantern/bladder cherry (*Physalis alkekengi franchetii*), 7, 28, 38, 99
Choisya, 9
Christmas arrangements, 32, 34, 36, 38, 41
Chrysanthemums (*Chrysanthemum* sp), 10, 38, 99, 108

Cinnamon sticks, 38, 87, 118
Circles, stem, making, 18, *see also* Garlands
Cladonia rangiferina, 22, 55, 60, 65, 87, 90, 131, 137
Cleaning arrangements, 11
Clematis, 10
Clematis seedheads (*Clematis* sp), 137
Consolida sp, 7, 24
Containers, preparing, 15–16
Copper beech (*Fagus sylvatica 'Cuprea'*), 9, 84, 94
Coral fern, 65
Cornflowers (*Centaurea cyranus*), 10
Cynara sp, 108; *Cynara scolymus*, 8, 32, 118, 126

Delphinium (*Delphinium* sp), 8, 24, 34, 44, 59, 76, 84, 92, 94, 96, 99, 122
Desiccants, 8
Dining table centrepieces, 81, 82
Dock (*Rumex* sp), 8
Dryandra (*Dryandra quercifolia*), 94
Drying methods, 7–10
Dryopteris sp, 65, 137
Dudinea (*Dudinea* sp), 62, 70, 81, 122
Dyer's saffron, *see* Safflower

Easter rabbit, 55
Echinops ritro, 122
Equipment, Basic, 13
Erica sp, 9, 132
Eryngium sp, 82
Eucalyptus (*Eucalyptus* sp), 9, 76, 132; Eucalyptus baby (*Eucalyptus* sp), 36, 72, 76, 84, 128; *Eucalyptus cinerea*, 43, 126
Everlasting/strawflowers (*Helichrysum* sp), 81, 110, 128; *Helichrysum bracteatum*, 26, 27, 32, 56, 62, 70, 82, 99, 102, 104, 108, 122; silver (*Helichrysum vestium*), 26, 27, 82, 92; Swan River (*Helichrysum manglesii*), 24, 25, 92; white cluster-flowered (*Helichrysum italicum*), 100

Fagus sylvatica, 24, 108; *Fagus sylvatica 'Cuprea'*, 9, 84, 94
Feather flower (*Verticordia* sp), 94, 122
Ferns (*Dryopteris* sp), 9, 10, 65, 137
Fescue grass (*Festuca* sp), 137
Festoon, 21
reel wire, 21
Fir-cone tree, 89
Fir cones, 28, 87
wiring, 19
Fireplace, 126, 128
Freesia, 10
Freeze drying, 8
Fruit, artificial, 41, 87, 118
Fungi, 30, 117, 118, 139
drying, 8
Garlands, 36, 96, 99, 100
bases, 17
Globe amaranth (*Gomphrena globosa*), 24, 92

Glycerine, preserving with, 9
Golden rod (*Solidago* sp), 9
Gomphrena globosa, 24, 92
Gramina sp, 66, 122
Grass (*Gramina* sp), 66, 122
Grass, hare's/pussy tail (*Lagurus ovatus*), 137
Grasses, drying, 8
Grimmia pulvinata, 34, 55
Gum nuts, 117
Gypsophila, 8, 10, 24, 59, 82, 108
Gypsophila rugosa, 26, 56, 81, 110, 122

Hair grass (*Aira* sp), 30
Hanging basket, 115
Hanging bunch, 102
Hat, 44
Hazel nuts, 65
Heathers (*Erica* sp), 9, 132
Hedera sp, 9, 22, 32, 38
Helianthus sp, 126
Helichrysum sp, 81, 110, 128
Helichrysum bracteatum, 26, 27, 32, 56, 62, 70, 82, 99, 102, 104, 108, 122
Helichrysum cordatum, 24
Helichrysum head, wiring, 18
Helichrysum italicum, 100
Helichrysum manglesii, 24, 25, 92
Helichrysum vestium, 26, 27, 82, 92
Helipterum, 7, 59, 94, 104, 122
Helipterum manglesii, 82
Helipterum/Rhodanthe sp, 128
Helipterum Sandfordii, 56, 69, 104
Hellebore, 10
Hogweed (*Heracleum sphondylium*), 8
Hoja leaves, 43, 139
Honesty (*Lunaria rediviva*), 59, 137
Hordeum sp, 26
Hydrangeas, 8, 9
Hydrangea, blue and green (*Hydrangea macrophylla*), 44, 62, 70, 72, 76, 81, 87, 94, 108, 110
Hydrangea, lace cap (*Hydrangea paniculata*), 10

Isolepsis, 140
Ivy (*Hedera* sp) 9, 22, 32, 38
artificial, 34
Ixodia sp, 94, 137

Jerusalem sage (*Phlomis fructicosa*), 9
Juncus sp, 43

Kangaroo paw (*Anigozanthos* sp), 108
Kangaroo paw, red (*Anigozanthos rufus*), 134

Lachnostachys sp, 108
Lady's mantle (*Alchemilla mollis*), 32, 99, 110
Lagurus ovatus, 137
Lamarcia, 65
Lapsana sp, 44
Larch (*Larix* sp), 28, 32, 34, 36, 38, 41
Larix sp, 28, 32, 34, 36, 38, 41

Larkspur (*Consolida* sp), 7, 24
Laurel (*Prunus laurocerasus*), 9
Lavender (*Lavendula spica*), 8, 34, 44, 60, 62,
    69, 70, 104, 110, 113, 115
Leaf dish, 46
Lepidium (*Lepidium ruderale*), 126
Leptospermum sp, 104
Leucodendron, 117
    Leucodendron plumosum, 65
    Leucodendron pubescens, 65
Lichen, 8
Lilies, 10
Limonium sp, 8, 10, 24, 26, 44, 56, 82, 87, 89,
    92, 134, 137
    Limonium sinuatum, 7, 24, 122
    Limonium suworowii, 24
Lonas inodora, 108
Lotus flowers (*Nelumbo lucifera*), 8, 34, 36,
    44, 65, 94, 99, 117, 118, 139, 140
Love-in-a-mist (*Nigella*), 10
    Nigella damascena, 62, 81, 94, 108, 122
    spiky green (*Nigella orientalis*), 66, 76, 94,
    126
Love-lies-bleeding (*Amaranthus* sp), 59, 94,
    122, 126
    green (*Amaranthus caudatus* 'Viridis'), 82,
    84, 108, 126
Lunaria rediviva, 59, 137

Magnolia leaves, 87, 107, 110
Mahonia, 9
Mantelpiece decorations, 32, 131–2
Marguerites (*Compositae* sp), 10
Marigolds (*Tagetes* sp), 10
Marjoram (*Origanum vulgare*), 62, 70, 72, 74,
    81, 84, 90, 104, 110
Melaleuca (*Melaleuca* sp), 24
Microwaving, 9
Mimosa/wattle (*Acacia*) 8
Miniatures, 122
Mirror frames, 117, 118
Moss, 8
    bun (*Grimmia pulvinata*), 34, 55
    flat (*Mnium* sp), 38, 78, 139
    reindeer, (*Cladonia rangiferina*), 22, 55, 60,
    65, 87, 90, 131, 137
    sack (*Mnium*), 34, 41, 52, 55, 60, 65, 78, 81,
    89, 107, 108, 131, 139
    sphagnum, 28, 32, 50, 89, 90, 92, 107, 115,
    120, 122, 125
    Spanish, 140

Names of plants, 10
Nelumbo lucifera, 8, 34, 36, 44, 65, 94, 99,
    117, 118, 139, 140
Nigella damascena, 62, 81, 94, 108, 122
Nigella orientalis, 66, 76, 94, 126
Nipplewort (*Lapsana* sp), 44
Nuts, 34, 118; gum , 117; hazel, 65; Mauritius,
    140; walnuts, 38

Oak twigs and leaves (*Quercus*), 100, 108
Onion (*Allium*), 137
    seedheads (*Allium*), 8
Oregano (*Origanum* sp), 62, 94, 126
Origanum vulgare, 62, 70, 72, 74, 81, 84, 90,
    104, 110
Oven drying, 9, 10

Palm spears (*Palmatus* sp), 36, 117, 134, 137
Pampas (*Cortaderia selloana*), 8

Pansies (*Viola* sp), 10
Papaver gigantum, 26, 126
Papaver somniferum, 22, 34, 36, 59, 66, 76, 87,
    110, 117
Pearl everlasting (Anaphalis), 70
Pedestals, 104, 107, 108
Peony (*Paeonia lactiflora*), 44, 56, 62, 70, 72,
    78, 84, 94, 110, 115, 126
    artificial, 126
Peppercorns, pink, 34, 118
Phalaris sp, 82
Phleum pratense, 65
Phlomis, 110
Phragmitis australis, 137
Physalis alkekengi franchetii, 7, 28, 38, 99
Pin oak (*Quercus palustris*), 9
Pine cones, 10
    Mexican white, 32, 108
    Scots (*Pinus sylvestris*), 34, 36, 38, 89
Polypogon, 65
Pom-pom trees, 90, 92
Poppy seedheads,
    golden (*Papaver gigantum*), 26, 126
    opium (*Papaver somniferum*), 22, 34, 36, 59,
    66, 76, 87, 110, 117
Posies, 84, 87
Pot pourri, 60, 62, 65
Pressing, 10
Primula, 10
Protea, 8; *Protea compacta*, 76; *Protea
    compacta* flat, 34; *Protea repens*, 65;
    Protea repens flat, 76, 99, 117

Quercus, 100, 108

Raffia, 20–1, 30
Rattan palm/wait-a-while vine (*Calamus* sp),
    34, 118
Reeds, bleached (*Phragmitis australis*), 137
Reel wire swag/festoon, 21
Ropes
    raffia, 20, 21
    swag/festoon, 21
Rose head, wiring, 18
Roses, 7, 24, 25, 50, 70, 125, 132
    artificial, 66, 126
    floribunda, 76, 87, 126
    hybrid tea, 34, 52, 62, 72, 74, 81, 84, 92, 94,
    96, 104, 110, 115, 120, 126
    leaves, 96
Rumex sp, 8
Ruscus, 122

Safflower (*Carthamus* sp), 36, 66
    orange-tipped/red-dyed/dyer's saffron
    (*Carthamus tinctorius*), 76, 99, 104, 126,
    128
Sage flowers (*Phlomis*), 110
Sago bush/Lachnostachys (*Lachnostachys* sp),
    108
Salix sp, 56, 94, 134, 137
Sandplain woody pear (*Xylomelum
    angustifolium*), 24, 137
Sea holly (*Eryngium* sp), 82
Sea lavender (*Limonium* sp), 8, 10, 24, 26, 56,
    82, 87, 92, 134, 137
Seacrest (*Helichrysum cordatum*), 24
Seed pods, 65, 118
Seedpod heads, 34
Semaphore sedge/rush (*Juncus* sp), 43
Senecio (*Senecio greyi*), 70, 82

Silver birch (*Betula pendula*), 100, 132
Silver dollar gum (*Eucalyptus cinerea*), 43, 126
Silver strawberry (*Leptospermum* sp), 89, 104
Six-rowed barley (*Hordeum* sp), 26
Snowdrops (*Galanthus* sp), 10
Sorghum/millet (*Gramina* sp), 66
South African daisies/Lonas (*Lonas inodora*),
    108
South Australian daisy (*Ixodia* sp), 94, 137
Spheres, making, 16
Sprays, 10
Statice (*Limonium* sp), 44, 89, 92
    Limonium sinuatum, 7, 24, 122
    Russian rat's tail (*Limonium suworowii*), 24,
    76
Stem circle, making, 18
Stems
    lengthening, 20
    wire, concealing, 19
Stirlingia (*Stirlingia latifolia*), 108, 134, 137
Stockists, 142
Sunflower (*Helianthus* sp), 126
Sunray (*Helipterum* sp), 59, 94, 104, 122
    white large-flowered (*Helipterum
    Rhodanthe* sp), 128
Sunray/Rhodanthe (*Helipterum manglesii*), 82
Swag, 94
    reel wire, 21
    rope, 21
Swan River everlasting (*Helipterum manglesii*),
    24, 25, 92
Sweet chestnuts, 65

Tassel flower (*Cacalia* sp), 82
Techniques, Basic, 14–21
Thistles (*Carlina acaulis*), 8, 78
Thistles (*Cynara* sp), 108
Thistles, globe (*Echinops ritro*), 122
Thyme, flowering (*Thymus* sp), 94
Timothy grass (*Phleum pratense*), 65
Ti tree/willow myrtle (*Agonis juniperina*), 24,
    92
Tree bark, 140; branches, 38; leaves, 10
Trees, 89, 90, 92, 107, 131, 139
Trinchinium australis, 137
Triticum, 22, 26, 30, 32, 34, 38, 66, 76, 82, 96,
    99, 102, 104, 128, 134

Verticordia sp, 94, 122
Vine stems, 46
Vines, pliable, 38

Walnuts, 38
Wheat (*Triticum*), 22, 30, 32, 66, 76, 82, 96,
    104
    bearded, 22, 26, 38, 99, 102, 128, 134
    bleached, 34
Wheat pots, 32
Wild oats (*Avena fatua*), 26, 104, 134
Willow, contorted (*Salix* sp), 56, 94, 134, 137
Willow myrtle, *see* Ti tree
Wiring, 18–20

Xylomelum angustifolium, 24, 137

Yarrow, (*Achillea* sp), 8, 122; *Achillea
    filipendulina*, 32, 43, 56, 76, 100, 104,
    108, 126; pink (*Achillea ptarmica*), 66

Zinnias, 10